SOCIAL PERSPECTIVES OF AGING

CHINA, AGING AND THEORY

SOCIAL PERSPECTIVES OF AGING

JASON L. POWELL, - SERIES EDITOR –

DEAN OF FACULTY, UNIVERSITY OF LIVERPOOL, UK

Aging, Theory and Globalization
Jason L. Powell
2011. ISBN: 978-1-61761-947-2
(Softcover)

Aging and Social Policy: A Foucauldian Excursion
Jason L. Powell
2011. ISBN: 978-1-61761-947-2
(Hardcover)

Aging in Perspective and the Case of China: Issues and Approaches
Sheying Chen and Jason L. Powell (Editors)
2011. ISBN: 978-1-61728-941-5
(Hardcover)

Social Welfare, Personal Budgets and Care: A Case Study
Jason L. Powell
2011. ISBN: 978-1-61209-332-1
(Softcover)

A Short Introduction to Social Theory
Jason L. Powell
2012. ISBN: 978-1-62100-928-3
(Softcover)

Aging, Gender and Crime
Jason L. Powell
2012. ISBN: 978-1-61942-150-9
(Softcover)

Exploring Policing, Crime and Society: A Brief but Critical Understanding
Jason L. Powell
2012. ISBN: 978-1-61942-001-4
(Softcover)

Foucault: Interdisciplinary Approaches
Jason L. Powell (Editor)
2012. ISBN: 978-1-61942-146-2
(Hardcover)

Foundations of Social Inquiry: A Brief Excursion
Jason L. Powell
2012. ISBN: 978-1-61942-004-5
(Softcover)

The Global Dynamics of Aging
Jason L. Powell and Sheying Chen (Editors)
2012. ISBN: 978-1-62100-936-8
(Hardcover)

The Sociology of Care: Exploring Theory, Policy and Practice – The Case of Aging
Jason L. Powell
2012. ISBN: 978-1-62100-697-8
(Softcover)

Understanding the Voluntary Sector: Critical Success Factors - A Case Study
Jason L. Powell
2012. ISBN: 978-1-62100-499-8
(Softcover)

China, Aging and Theory
Jason L. Powell
2012. ISBN: 978-1-62100-915-3
(Softcover)

SOCIAL PERSPECTIVES OF AGING

CHINA, AGING AND THEORY

JASON L. POWELL

Nova Science Publishers, Inc.
New York

For permission to use material from this book please contact us:
Telephone 631-231-7269; Fax 631-231-8175
Web Site: http://www.novapublishers.com

Library of Congress Cataloging-in-Publication Data

China, aging, and theory / editor, Jason L. Powell.
p. cm.
Includes index.
ISBN 978-1-62100-915-3 (softcover)
1. Aging--China. 2. Older people--Government policy--China. 3. Older people--China--Social conditions. 4. Older people--China--Economic conditions. 5. Gerontology. I. Powell, Jason L., 1971-
HQ1064.C6C456 2011
305.260951--dc23

2011038594

Published by Nova Science Publishers, Inc. † New York

CONTENTS

PREFACE

This book provides a theoretical critique and analysis of the development and consolidation of power in China as it applies to aging. In seeking to deal with this increased proportion of older people, Chinese state policy seeks to introduce ways of reducing the fiscal burden of aging upon the state, and, indeed, upon those many families who have been markedly affected by the modernization process. This book, however, fundamentally questions the assumption that populational policies in the Chinese state are unbiased in their social practices with older people. The book explores new topics and examplars of aging in China, grounded in and drawing from developments in social theory, i.e., Foucauldian theory and postmodernism.

Chapter 1

INTRODUCTION

This book provides a theoretical critique and analysis of the development and consolidation of power in China as it applies to aging. As shown in previous works (eg., Chen and Powell, 2012; Li Yongping and Peng Xizhe, 2000; Powell and Cook, 2010; Zhai Zhenwu, 2000), China's aging population is growing dramatically as a proportion of the total Chinese population, in part due to the success of the Communist Party of China (CPC) in delivering economic modernization to much of the population, but also due to the knock-on effects of the Single Child Family Program, which has been in place, to a greater or lesser degree, since the 1970s, thus reducing the proportion of younger people within China (Murray, 1998; Powell 2011).

In seeking to deal with this increased proportion of elderly people, Chinese state policy can be seen as being essentially rational and fair-minded, seeking to introduce ways of reducing the fiscal burden of aging upon the state, and indeed upon those many families who have been markedly affected by the modernization process. This book, however, fundamentally questions the assumption that populational policies in the Chinese state are unbiased in their social practices with older people. Indeed, narratives of social policy in Western culture have focused on old age with strong emphasis on the reform of social welfare (Biggs & Powell 2001).

In the case of China, the process of political and economic reform was imposed in a top-down manner via "democratic centralism" supported by highly stretched demographic arguments (Powell & Cook 2010). These reforms purportedly offered the promise of greater choice and narratives of "people power" for both families and older people through the introduction of the market ethos (market socialism or "socialism with Chinese characteristics") into areas traditionally controlled, directly or indirectly, by the State (Powell & Cook 2010). The huge costs of welfare provision in recent decades have been subsidized by them via the lending programs of the state banking system.

In order to theoretically interrogate this, the following chapters provide rich insights into how aging in China can be theorized. Chapter 2 illustrates how Chinese society placed elderly people on a pedestal. It was part of the filial duties imposed by Confucianism to care for one's parents when they were old. Today, however, that old order in China is breaking down, at the very time that the proportion of the elderly is increasing as the "superaging" of the population takes place. When coupled with the decrease in births associated with the People's Republic Single Child Family Program, plus the lack of a developed welfare system, the increased number of elderly is giving rise to serious concerns among Chinese policy makers. While not seeking to minimize the issues concerning the frail elderly, this chapter presents a different "take" on aging, focusing on the "active elderly." The chapter aims to dispel the stereotypes of the elderly; an alternative discourse is possible, in which the elderly are viewed as a resource, not as a problem. This has implications for the epistemological development of gerontology.

Chapter 3 focuses on gerontological issues in China, where the older people have become a rapidly expanding proportion of the population. While resources do need to be targeted on the vulnerable older people, the presumption that older people as a whole are an economic and social burden must be questioned. This is an ageist view that needs to be combated by identifying how bio-medical views on aging seep into policy spaces in China, positioning negative perceptions of aging as both an individual and populational problem. The chapter then moves to observe the implications of bio-medicine for older people in China in terms of "vulnerable" aging, but deconstructs such "fixed" explanations by juxtaposing *active aging* as a key narrative that epitomizes "declining to decline" as espoused by bio-medical sciences.

Chapter 4 suggests that the Chinese state is not instigating narratives of "choice," but rather of technology for collective control. Thus, there are two dimensions which are particularly important to the trajectory of this paper. Firstly, there is the use of a Foucauldian perspective to understand and explain the relationship between the Chinese state and elderly people. Secondly, there is the notion of "power" and its relevance to the consolidation of a narrative communicated by the Chinese state, which provides surveillance over a populational group: a Chinese "elderly population."

Chapter 5 alerts social scientists to the partial nature of the narratives supplied by policy in China, which affects perceptions of older people. The simplifying role of policy discourse tends to highlight certain, politically valued, aspects of experience to the exclusion of other possibilities. The chapter assesses what discourses are most likely to be reflected in Chinese state policy-sponsored research.

In chapter 6, we consider the question of trust and how different conceptions of trust provide epistemic insights into the conditions upon which trust operates in China. For without trust, state activities in China reliant on cooperation between individuals and communities with future orientated expectations have no satisfactory basis on which they might be established.

Finally, chapter 7, the concluding chapter, attempts to "go beyond" China and focuses on comparative analysis with other countries in Asia. Asia itself has the fastest increasing aging population in the world.

It is hoped that the book raises questions about the inter-relationship between China, aging and theory. It is hoped that the book will be both rewarding and challenge your thoughts on China, aging and social theory.

Chapter 2

ACTIVITY, AGING AND CHINA

INTRODUCTION

To understand older people and their relationship to the Chinese state, we must recognize that the historical meaning of old age changes in response to a wide variety of social, economic, political, cultural and inter-personal conditions. Social policies are both an attempt to shape and are themselves shaped by these meanings. In the United Kingdom, for example, much politicking has surrounded older people, including controversies over pensions, care and proposed legal reforms concerning employment. In western societies, older people have been viewed in "burden" and "dependent" terms. Conversely, pre-modern or traditional Chinese society placed elderly people on a pedestal (Cook, 2001). They were valued for their accumulated knowledge, their position within the extended family, and the sense of history and identity which they helped the family to develop (Murray, 1998).

It was part of the duties imposed by Confucianism to care for one's parents when they were old, so that when you too were old your children would in turn care for you. Reciprocity was a key feature; son, fathers, mothers and daughters had rights as well as responsibilities. However, today, in the "new" China, that old order in China is breaking down, as Powell and Cook (2000), for example, have shown, due to the dramatic changes that the People's Republic has witnessed in recent decades. There is, for example, increased migration to cities by younger people, leaving the elderly as a "residual" population in rural areas, and dislocating, literally and figuratively, the traditional links between generations. Also, increased prosperity and good health care has markedly increased average lifespan, from 47.1 years in 1960 to 68.6 years in 1993 (Tang, 1999). Life expectancy at birth reached an estimated 69.0 years for males and 73.0 years for females by the year 2000 (*Britannica Book of the Year, 2001*).

Active Aging in China I : Politics, Power and Representations of Old Age in CCP

For the Chinese Communist Party (CCP), which rules China, the view of the elderly has been highly variable, and sometimes contradictory. For much of the time the Party has viewed the elderly essentially as dependents, to be looked after by the work unit, or family, as the case may be. Yet within the Party hierarchy, the elderly assumed a major role, either within its formal structures such as the Politburo, or when ostensibly retired from these organizations informally via more shadowy "advisory" bodies, which retain great power. The CCP itself has a tradition of the elderly being active within its power structures, and its great leaders, Mao Zedong, Zhou Enlai and Deng Xiaoping, worked to a very great age, into their eighties. Two examples illustrate this point.

Firstly, there were Mao's activities during the mid-1960s. Born in 1893, he was by then in semi-retirement, partly shunted aside by the CCP after the failures of the Great Leap Forward. In 1965 he orchestrated a spectacular propaganda coup by swimming in the Yangtze River at the venerable age of 72, accompanied by photographers in motor launches. Where he swam, off Wuhan, the river is nearly two miles wide and beset by difficult currents. Mao, however, was always a strong swimmer. Moreover, provided the swimmer follows the current downstream, at an angle to the river, and swims in the warm summer waters, great distance can be achieved. The impact on China, and indeed on overseas opinion, was startling. For home consumption, "this exercise at such a place was no doubt partly designed to refute the fears and superstitions of the people who still dreaded the 'River Dragon,' which devours swimmers" (Fitzgerald, 1976, p. 138). Mao built on this success to launch the Great Proletarian Cultural Revolution the following year, having reconfirmed his cult status.

In a less dramatic, but no less important, vein was the role of Deng Xiaoping and others of the "eight elders" during Tiananmen in 1989. Born in 1904, Deng was thus 85 at this time, and some of the other elders were even older. They came together to express their concerns over what they viewed as too soft a response by the Politburo Standing Committee to the ongoing student protest in the square. They still had power and used it firstly on May 18th to meet with the Standing Committee (minus Zhao Ziyang, then General Secretary of the CCP and a noted reformer, known to be sympathetic to many of the views held by the students) and the leaders of the key Central Military Commission to order that Beijing be put under martial law. Zhao Ziyang was ousted, and on May 21st "Deng Xiaoping convened the Party Elders to take charge since the younger generation of leaders seemed unable to manage" (Nathan and Link, 2001, p. 223). They agreed on Jiang Zemin, the current leader of the PRC, as the replacement for Zhao Ziyang at a meeting on May 27th. Finally, on June 2nd, the fateful decision was taken to clear the square by force, and on June 4, 1989, the terrible die was cast at Tiananmen, despite Deng Xiaoping's instructions to avoid bloodshed in the square itself.

Deng Xiaoping's image in the West as a small "cuddly uncle" who wore ten-gallon hats during his visits to the U.S.A. and was behind the reform period in China, was transformed to the "Butcher of Beijing" for his part in Tiananmen. However, he revived his tainted reputation as far as the West was concerned, or at least Western businessmen, via his famous South China tour in 1992, at an even more advanced age (Cook and Murray, 2001). During this tour, allegedly under armed guard, Deng courageously backed further opening up in China, and this gave the green light to a massive foreign investment in the country, to a "China Fever" which led to Deng Xiaoping receiving *Time's* "Man of the Year" accolade in 1992. By then he was 87 and remained in remarkably rude health given that he was well-known as a chain smoker right up to his death at the age of 93 in February 1997. The CCP contains, therefore, a tradition of service and work to an advanced age.

Active Aging in China II: The Aging Population

There have been calls for governments across the world to regard "their burgeoning aging populations as 'invisible resources' instead of viewing the elderly as unwitting victims of poverty, disease and social exclusion" (Tang, 2001a). He noted in his speech that many people view the elderly as a problem rather than as a resource. Many elderly people for example, continue to be major income providers for their families, or act as care givers for others. Zeng (2001) called, therefore, for governments to fully credit the social contributions of the elderly via new social development measures. We fully support this perspective on the elderly. Moving away from a broad-brush categorization of the elderly as a "frail," "severely disabled"'or "incapacitated" group enables a more sensitive interaction with elderly people. Ideally, policy responses would move towards interacting with older people as individuals genuinely empowered to lead fulfilling lives that are as active as possible.

Within the People's Republic of China there are genuine concerns about improving the well-being of the elderly, as shown in the latest five-year plan, for example, as well as a range of recent measures to improve the profile of the elderly and the attention paid to them (Guo, 2001;Tang 2001b; Zeng 2001). The increased longevity points to the progress already made within the country. We would argue that, as far as possible, policies should build on those introduced in the 1980s to encourage physical and gentle exercise, of the types illustrated above by Yu. There should also be a renewal of the ancient system of respect for the elderly, albeit without the fear or deference which was often found in traditional society. To value the elderly, to involve them wherever possible, and to view them as a resource rather than as a problem would seem to us to be the way forward, in China and elsewhere. Hence, we are also sensitized to the concept of living with multiple narratives that impinge on viewing old age in many dimensions.

AGING IN CHINA: LIVING WITH MULTIPLE NARRATIVES

Each phase of Chinese society and active aging leaves a legacy. Moreover, policy development is uneven and subject to local emphasis and elision, which means that it is quite possible for different, even conflicting narratives of later life to coexist in different parts of the policy system within China. Each period generates a discourse that can legitimize the lives of older people in particular ways and, as their influence accrues, create the potential for entering into multiple narrative streams (i.e., as political leaders and as a population).

Also, both policy discourses share a deep coherence, which may help to explain their co-existence. Such narrative streams offer a partial view of aging while downloading risk and responsibility onto aging identities (Chen and Powell 2012).

If the analysis outlined above is accepted, then it is possible to see contemporary Chinese society addressing diverse aspects of older people in differing and contradictory ways. Contradictory narratives for active aging are in a landscape that is at the same time increasingly blurred in terms of roles and relationships and split-off in terms of narrative coherence and consequences for aging identity. Indeed, in a future of complex and multiple policy agendas, it would appear that a narrative of social inclusion through active aging can coexist with one emphasizing carer obligation and state surveillance (Powell and Cook, 2000). Such a co-existence may occasionally become inconvenient at the level of public rhetoric. However, at an experiential and ontological level, that is to say at the level of the daily lives of older adults, the implications may become particularly acute. Multiple co-existing policy narratives may become a significant source of risk to identity maintenance within the aging identities in China (Chen and Powell 2012).

One has to imagine a situation in which later lives are lived, skating on a surface of legitimizing discourse. For everyday intents and purposes, this surface supplies the ground on which one can build an aging identity, related to other family members and the immediate community. However, there is always the possibility of slipping, of being subject to trauma or transition. Serious slippage will provoke being thrown onto a terrain that had previously been hidden, an alternative narrative of aging with entirely different premises, relationship expectations and possibilities for personal expression.

Policy narratives, however, are also continually breaking down and fail to achieve hegemony as they encounter lived experience. Indeed, it could be argued that a continuous process of re-constitution takes place via the play of competing narratives. When we are addressing the issue of older people's identity in later life we can usefully note Foucault's (1977) contention that there has been a growth in attempts to control national populations through discourses of normality, but at the same time this has entailed increasing possibilities for self-government, another way of contextualizing "active aging" (Chen and Powell 2012).

Part of the attractiveness of thinking in terms of narrative is that populational policies tell us stories that we don't necessarily have to believe and are the opening of a critical distance between description and intention. Policy narratives describe certain, often idealized, states of affairs. Depicting them as stories, rather than as realities, allows the interrogation of the space between that description and experience.

CONCLUSION

What does this examination of discourse and everyday narratives of aging tell us about China and constructions of identity, and what are the lessons for future applied research?

Firstly, we are alerted to the partial nature of the narratives supplied by policy in China, which affects perceptions of older people. The simplifying role of policy discourse tends to highlight certain, politically valued, aspects of experience to the exclusion of other possibilities. These are also the discourses most likely to be reflected in Chinese state policy-sponsored research.

Secondly, the inclusion of certain roles, activities and age bands in populational policy discourse in China has a legitimizing role. In other words, it not only sanctions the direction of resources and the action of state professionals, as important though as that is. It also contributes to the legitimized identities afforded to people in later life. This includes at least two factors key to aging identity: the creation of social spaces in which to perform aging roles and be recognized as such, and, the supply of material with which explicit yet personal narratives of self can be made.

Thirdly, a significant element in the "riskiness" of building aging identities under contemporary conditions may arise from the existence of multiple policy discourses that personal narratives, of self, the Chinese State and relations between the two, have to negotiate. Research on the management of identity should, then, be sensitized to the multiple grounds on which identity might be built and the potential sources of conflict and uncertainty.

Fourthly, attention should be paid to the relationship between tacit and explicit influences on identity management in later-life in China. The multiple sources for building stories "to live by" and the tension between legitimizing discourses and alternative narratives of self and family would suggest that identities are managed at different levels, for different audiences and at different levels of awareness. There are implications here for both the conceptualization of old age and policy relations and for the practice of research.

In summary, we have argued that future developments in policy analysis in China will have to take both tacit and explicit themes in populational policy into account as relating to elderly people. They will also have to more closely examine the relationship between personal story-making and formal public policy discourses in China. Policies provide narrative templates within which certain categories of people or groups are encouraged to live out their lives. However, this legitimized performance may differ significantly from an individual's or group's everyday experience of that same role, function, or social space, leading to conflict between different levels of narrative. We are left in the end with a question: how far will it be possible for aging families to use opportunities for positive growth and resistance, and how far does that growth go beyond dominant representations of later life epitomized by bio-medical models of aging? The next chapter focuses its attention to that.

Chapter 3

CHINA, GERONTOLOGY AND THE BIO-MEDICALIZATION OF AGING

Social scientists around the globe are increasingly concerned about the rising numbers of older people in their society. There are worries about the inadequacy of pension funds, of growing pressures on welfare systems, and on the inability of shrinking numbers of younger people to carry the burden of their elders. This article focuses on such gerontological issues in China, where the older people have become a rapidly expanding proportion of the population. While resources do need to be targeted on the vulnerable older people, the presumption that older people as a whole are an economic and social burden must be questioned (Chen and Powell 2012). This is an ageist view that needs to be combated by locating how bio-medical views on aging seep into policy spaces in China that position negative perceptions of aging as both individual and populational problems. The article then moves to observe the implications of bio-medicine for older people in China in terms of "vulnerable" aging, but deconstruct such "fixed" explanations by juxtaposing *active aging* as a key narrative that epitomizes "declining to decline," as espoused by bio-medical sciences.

Introduction: From "Global Aging" to "Aging in China"

There is no doubt that in many societies around the globe older people are a growing proportion of the global population (Krug 2002). The age structure of the global population is changing from one in which younger people predominated to a society in which people in later life constitute a substantial proportion of the total population. While the biological and psychological models of aging inscribe it as an "inevitable" and "universal" process, an aging population is neither (Phillipson, 1998). Transformations in the age profile of a population are a response to political and economic structures. A major concern for organizations such as the United Nations and World Bank focuses on the number of such "dependent" older people in world society (Krug 2002).

Indeed, older people in particular constitute a large section of populations in global aging. In relation to public services that have to be paid for by "younger" working people, the percentage of the population has been used to signify such "burdensome" numbers. Not only are older people seen as dependent, but also children under school-leaving age and people over the retirement age. Dependency rates—that is, the number of dependents related to those of working age—altered little over the twentieth century and yet the notion of the "burden" group retains its legitimacy. The reason there has been so little change during a period of so-called rapid aging populations is that there has been a fall in the total fertility rate (the average number of children that would be born to each woman if the current age-specific birth rates persisted throughout her child-bearing life) (Phillipson, 1998).

Changes in the age structures of all societies also affect total levels of labor force participation in society, because the likelihood that an individual will be in the labor force varies systematically by age. Concurrently, global population aging is projected to lead to lower proportions of the population in the labor force in highly industrialized nations, threatening both productivity and the ability to support an aging population (Powell, 2009). Coupled with rapid growth in the young adult population in Third World countries, the World Bank (1994) foresees growing "threats" to international stability, pitting different demographic-economic regions against one another. That the United Nations (2002) views the relationship between aging populations and labor force participation with panic recognizes important policy challenges, including the need to reverse recent trends toward decreasing labor force participation of workers in late-middle and old age despite mandatory retirement in both Western and Eastern countries such as the UK (Jackson and Powell, 2001) and China (Chen and Powell, 2011).

Notwithstanding this, in China there is also an ongoing huge increase in the aging population that replicates global trends. It can be seen that the percentage of the aging population has increased from just over 4.4 percent to just under 7 percent from 1953 to 2000 (Cook and Murray 2001). It can be noted that the increase has not been constant, reflecting the negative impact of the Great Leap Forward and the successive famines upon the demographic profile, shown in the results of the 1964 Census.

Since that latter date, the percentage of the elderly has nearly doubled, while the actual numbers have more than tripled, being approximately 3.6 times that of 1964 by the year 2000. By 2000, there were 88 million Chinese aged 65 or over, compared to just under 25 million in 1964, an increase of 63 million plus in 36 years.

As is well known, China's population policy, most usually referred to as the Single Child Family Program (although some Chinese commentators regard the phrase as a misnomer, given that more than one child is possible within a number of situations), has led to a rapid deceleration in the birth rate, which was only 13.38 per thousand in 2001, compared to 21.06 in 1990 and 18.25 in 1978 (Cook and Murray 2001).

This controversial policy, lambasted and praised in equal measure depending on perspective, has meant a rapid expansion in the number of single-child only households at the very same time that the proportion of the elderly has also increased, as a new era of prosperity has reached many households in China.

Estimates suggest that up to 300 million less people have been born as a result of this process of state intervention, but Murray (2004) has built on the earlier work of D.G. Johnson and others to suggest that improved living standards via modernization would have led to the same outcome voluntarily as the growing numbers of urban dwellers in particular chose to reduce their family size. This last point hints at the important spatial dimension of demographic change in China. There is on the one hand a marked contrast between urban and rural life in China and, closely related to this, a marked contrast between Eastern China and Western China (Cook and Powell, 2007). It is in the heavily urbanized "Gold Coast" of the Eastern Seaboard that China's spatial transformation is most dramatic, with fast-expanding cities being especially concentrated in the Pearl River delta of the Southeast and the Yangtse Delta in Central East China (Cook and Murray 2001).

Hence, it is not simply that the Chinese government has belatedly recognized "the greying" of populational constructions and policy implications, it is that they continue to look for knowledge of aging as the power to define old age as a social problem in terms of dualistic distinctions between deviancy and normality. An aging population, like that of an individual being studied by bio-medical models, is seen as a "burden" problem in terms of economic management of Eastern (and Western) economies.

It could be argued when looking at the effects of a so-called "demographic time bomb" across the U.S., Europe, and Asia, that it may have been grossly exaggerated.

Such old age, therefore, has been perceived negatively via a process of "ageism"—stereotyping older people simply because of their chronological age. Ageist stereotypes, such as "aging populations," act to stigmatize and consequently marginalize older people and differentiate them from groups across the life-course who are not labeled "old" (Bytheway, 1993).

One of the ways to interpret social aging as being a categorization, whether it be in individual or populational terms, is through the use of theorizing what it means to age in society, that is, concerns and social issues associated with aging and the ways in which these themes are influenced and at the same time influence the society in which people live. Thus, to understand the process of aging, looking through the lens of the "sociological imagination," is not to see it as an individualized problem, but rather as a societal issue that is faced by both First World and Third World nations as a whole.

In supporting this latter view, there is a need to focus on how populational discourses of aging in China are influenced and reinforced by bio-medical models of aging that help drive perceptions of older people as a burdensome group.

WHERE DOES THE AMBIVALENCE TO AGING COME FROM?

There are important implications for how aging is viewed, not only in terms of global aging but more specifically of China and the arrangement of political and economic structures that create and sanction social policies grounded in knowledge bases of "burdensome" populations (cf Powell, 2001). Such knowledge bases are focused on: one, "biological aging," which refers to the internal and external physiological changes that take place in the individual body and, two, psychological aging, understood as the developmental changes in mental functioning—emotional and cognitive capacities.

Bio-medical theories of aging can be distinguished from social construction of aging by focusing on: (1) the bio-psychological constituent of aging, and (2) on how aging has been socially constructed. One perspective is driven from "within" and privileges the expression from inner to outer worlds. The other is much more concerned with the power of external structures that shape individuality. In essence, this social constructionism poses the problem from the perspective of an observer looking in, while the biomedical model takes the stance of inside the individual looking out (Powell and Biggs, 2000). There has long been a tendency in matters of aging and old age to reduce the social experience of aging to its biological dimension from which is derived a set of normative "stages," which over-determine the experience of aging.

Accordingly, being "old," for example, would primarily be an individualized experience of adaptation to inevitable physical and mental decline and of preparation for death. The paradox of course is that the homogenizing of the experience of old age, which the reliance on the biological dimension of old age entails, is in fact one of the key elements of the dominant discourse on aging and old age.

It is interesting that comparative historical research on aging in Eastern culture highlights an alternative perception of aging: 18th century China highlighted a rather different path to the conceptualization of aging as a scientific process developed by western rationality. For example, Cook and Powell (2003) observe that traditional Chinese society placed older people on a pedestal. They were valued for their accumulated knowledge, their position within the extended family, and the sense of history and identity that they helped the family to develop (Murray, 1998). Respect for elderly people was an integral part of Confucian doctrine, especially for the family patriarch.

This was a view that was also prevalent in Ancient Greece with the notions of "respect" for older people, especially regarding gendered issues of patriarchy (cf Bytheway, 1993). Prior to industrialization, in India there was a bestowment that older people had responsible leadership roles and powerful decision-making positions because of their vast "experience," "wisdom" and "knowledge" (Katz, 1996).

It seems with the instigation of Western science and rationality, aging began to be viewed in a different more problematic context than in the Confucian doctrine of aging epitomized in China and issues of respect for aging in India. Martin Heidegger (1971) makes the similar point when he spoke of the Westernization of the world through the principles of Western science and language.

Indeed, the technological developments due to industrialization, Westernization, and urbanization—under the purview of a distorted form of modernity—have neglected these statuses of aging by downgrading its conceptualization. Part of understanding individuality in Western culture, the birth of "science" gave legitimate credibility to a range of bio-medical disciplines which were part of its umbrella. In particular, the bio-medical model has become one of the most controversial yet powerful of both disciplines and practice with regard to aging (Powell and Biggs, 2000).

The bio-medical model represents the contested terrain of decisions reflecting both normative claims and technological possibilities. "Bio-medicine" refers to medical techniques that privilege a biological and psychological understanding of the human condition and rely upon "scientific assumptions" that position attitudes of aging in society for their existence and practice. Hence, scientific medicine is based on the biological and psychological sciences. Some doctrines of the biomedical model more closely reflect the basic sciences while others refer to the primary concern of medicine, namely diseases located in the human body. Most important is that these beliefs hold together, thereby reinforcing one another and forming a coherent orientation toward the mind and body. Indeed, the mind-body dualism had become the location of regimen and control for emergence of science in a positivist methodological search for objective "truth." The end product of this process in the West is the "biomedical model."

In this sense, bio-medicine is based on the biological and psychological sciences. Some doctrines of the biomedical model more closely reflect the basic sciences while others refer to the primary concern of medicine, namely diseases located in the human body. Most important is that these beliefs hold together, thereby reinforcing one another and forming a coherent whole (Powell, 2001). By developing an all-encompassing range of bio-medical discourses, many forms of social injustice could be justified as "natural," inevitable and necessary for the successful equilibrium of the social whole, such as mandatory retirement and allocation of pensions (Phillipson, 1998).

Bio-medical gerontology is a fundamental domain where medical discourses on aging have become located, and this is very powerful in articulating "truths" about aging. Under the guise of science and its perceived tenets of value-freedom, objectivity and precision (Biggs, 1993), bio-medical gerontology has a cloth of legitimacy. Biological and psychological characteristics associated with aging have been used to construct scientific representations of aging in modern society. The characteristics of biological aging, as associated with loss of skin elasticity, wrinkled skin, hair loss or physical frailty, perpetuate powerful assumptions that help facilitate attitudes and perceptions of aging. It may be argued that rather than provide a scientific explanation of aging, such an approach homogenizes the experiences of aging by suggesting these characteristics are universal, natural and inevitable. These assumptions are powerful in creating a knowledge base for health and social welfare professionals who work with older people in particular medical settings, such as a hospital or general doctors' surgery and also for social workers (Powell 2009).

These new forms of social regulation were also reflected in the family and the community. Hence, modern systems of social regulation have become increasingly blurred and wide-ranging (Powell, 2009). Increasingly, modern society regulated the populational construct by sanctioning the knowledge and practices of the new human sciences—particularly psychology and biology. These are called gerontological "epistemes," which are "the total set of relations that unite at a given period, the discursive practices that give rise to epistemological figures, sciences and possibly formalized systems" (Foucault, 1972: 191). The "psy" complex or bio-medical epistemes refer to the network of ideas about the "nature" of individuals, their perfectability, the reasons for their behavior and the ways they may be classified, selected and controlled. It aims to manage and improve individuals by the manipulation of their qualities and attributes and is dependent upon scientific knowledge and professional interventions and expertise. Human qualities are seen as measurable and calculable and thereby can be changed and improved. The new human sciences had as their central aim the prediction of future behavior (Powell, 2009).

Powell and Biggs (2000) suggest that a prevailing ideology of ageism manifests itself in the bio-medical model via its suggestion that people with such biological traits have entered a spiral of decay, decline and deterioration. Along with this goes certain assumptions about the ways in which people with outward signs of aging are likely to think and behave. For example, there are assumptions that "older people are poor drivers" or that older people have little interest in relationships that involve sexual pleasure, wich are all explained away by "decline" and "deterioration" master narratives that comprise an aging culture. The effects of the "decline" and "decay" analogies can be most clearly seen in the dominance of medico-technical solutions to the problems that aging and even an "aging population" (Phillipson, 1998) are thought to pose. Here, the bio-medical model has both come to colonize notions of age and reinforce ageist social prejudices to the extent that "decline" has come to stand for the process of aging itself (Powell, 2001).

Estes and Binney (1989 cited in Powell, 2001) have used the expression "biomedicalization of aging," which has two closely related narratives: (1) the social construction of aging as a medical problem, and (2) ageist practices and policies growing out of thinking of aging as a medical problem. They suggest:

> Equating old age with illness has encouraged society to think about aging as pathological or abnormal. The undesirability of conditions labeled as sickness or illness transfer to those who have these conditions, shaping the attitudes of the persons themselves and those of others towards them. Sick role expectations may result in such behaviors as social withdrawal, reduction in activity, increased dependency and the loss of effectiveness and personal control—all of which may result in the social control of the elderly through medical definition, management and treatment (Estes and Binney, 1989, quoted in Powell, 2001: 119).

These authors highlight how individual lives and physical and mental capacities that were thought to be determined solely by biological and psychological factors, are, in fact, heavily influenced by social environments in which people live. These influences remain invisible to the bio-medical approach because they stem from societal interaction before becoming embedded and recognizable as an "illness" in the aging body of the person. For example, in the "sociology of emotions" the excursion of inquiry has proposed that "stress" is not only rooted in individualistic emotional responses but also regulated, classified, and shaped by social norms of western culture (Powell and Biggs, 2000).

This type of research enables the scope of aging to be broadened beyond bio-medical individualistic accounts of the body. On this basis alone, sociology invites us to recognize that aging is not only a socially constructed problem by bio-medical sciences but also the symptomatic, deep manifestation of underlying relations of power and inequality that cut across and through age, class, gender, disability and sexuality (Powell and Biggs, 2000; Powell, 2001).

At this level of analysis, sociology addresses bio-medicine as one of the elements of social control and domination legitimated through power/knowledge of "experts" (Powell and Biggs, 2000). Such expert formation has also been labeled as ageist (Bytheway, 1993). Agism is where the assumptions made about old age are negative andolder people are treated not as individuals but as a homogenous groupthat can be discriminated against (Bytheway, 1993).

Chinese society uses age categories to divide this ongoing process into stages or segments of life. These life stages are socially constructed rather than inevitable. Aging, too, is a production of social category. At any point of life span, age simultaneously denotes a set of social constructs, defined by the norms specific to a given society at a specific point in history. Thus, a specific period of life-infancy, childhood, adolescence, adulthood, middle age or old age-is influenced by the structural entities of a given society. Therefore, aging is not to be considered the mere product of biological-psychological function, but rather a consequence of sociocultural factors and subsequent life-chances. Indeed, society has a number of culturally and socially defined notions of what Phillipson (1998) calls the "stages of life." However, a fundamental question is how bio-medical gerontology has stabilized itself with a positivist discourse that not only reflects history, but also the total preoccupation with the "problems" of aging that have important implications for older people and health lifestyles in China.

Bio-Medicine, Family Care, and Aging: Implications for China

The dominant bio-medical discourse of aging in China dwells on the processes of physical deterioration associated with becoming older. In this perspective, the aging body has to deal with increased levels of incapacity, both physical and mental, and becomes increasingly dependent on younger others for sustenance and survival. It is the family, through informal care, that has to provide care of older people who may have illnesses, according to the Law on the Rights and Interests of the Elderly, introduced by the PRC in 1996. The bio-medical problematization of aging has secreted wider questions of power and inequality; occidental modernity is especially influential. A powerful discourse is thus developed which follows that of the West, via notions of "social inclusion" and "family care" and the all-important role of the consumer in buying products for the elderly, from disability aids to private pensions (Powell and Cook, 2001). The latter suggests that this process constructs the aging body as a site of surveillance by the Chinese state, constructing them as, following Foucault, objects of power and knowledge in which "it's your age" is the prevailing authority response to the elderly "customer."

Powell and Cook (2001) have further noted that older people will be increasingly probed for social, psychological and economic factors such as "frailty" or "expected level of supervision." "There are indications, for example, that where care homes are provided, these are for the more active elderly, rather than those in greatest need" (Powell and Cook, 2001: 7).

In light of these and other issues the PRC government is attempting to change the ways in which the elderly are perceived, via campaign slogans such as "Respect the elderly" and "People first." The former campaign seeks to encourage younger people to visit the elderly on a regular basis in order to reduce the sense of isolation that the elderly can feel, to look out for their needs out on the streets and to generally raise awareness of the situation of older people. There is a resonance here with ancient Confucian tradition in which the elderly were venerated. There have also been attempts to encourage younger people to think about "healthy aging," but this is meant in terms of ensuring that they themselves have adequate financial provision as they age. *"People first" is the attempt to recognize that "aging is an individual-specific process" and that "a functional healthcare system for the elderly should integrate all aspects of care ... emphasizing and fulfilling individual needs and preferences"* (CD, 2004).

Older people in rural areas are more likely to have to face emigration of their children to the cities as China's urbanization proceeds apace. This can leave them physically and socially isolated in a remote rural area, no longer able to rely upon their family to look after them in their old age, as was once the tradition.

Indeed, as social norms and values change, younger people may no longer be willing, even when they are able, to support elderly parents, and in recent years the law has been used to take children to court in order to force them to support their parents. For example, a new law came into force on October 1, 1996 on "The Rights and Interests of the Elderly" that explicitly states that: "The elderly shall be provided for mainly by their families, and their family members shall care for and look after them" (Du and Tu, 2000).

Notwithstanding the legal process, at its most extreme, the concerns of elderly people are expressed via suicide—gerontocide. The elderly can struggle in the face of the massive social changes that China is facing, and the abandonment of the tradition in which they themselves would have looked after their own parents and grandparents. They may feel so stressed and alienated that suicide seems the preferred option.

For example, a 76 year old man blew himself up in a courtroom in protest during a case against his family, who had offered only 350 Yuan a month to support him when 600 Yuan was required (8 Yuan = 1 USD) (Cook and Murray 2001). In a society of rapid transformation, older people in particular may be vulnerable to the sense of abandonment within a more materialistic and selfish new world epitomized by the forces of global capitalism and seeping impingement into day to day living of older people in China.

Declining to Decline — Active Aging?

At the other end of the scale is the active elderly, probably the ideal state for all elderly people. Briefly, older people traditionally were more likely to be active within rural areas of China, in part because they had to be in order to maintain their livelihood. This particular tradition continues today; official data for the 1990s showed that 26 percent of people in rural areas still depended on their own labor earnings compared to only 7 percent in urban areas.

This is not about advocating that elderly people should have to work to continue to earn a living, but we are suggesting that an active lifestyle be promoted where possible. In the cities of China today, it is heartening to see the colonization of open space throughout the hours of daylight, and even into the evening, by the elderly who are engaged in a wide variety of activities, from the traditional (such as taijiquan and qigong), walking one's pet bird, traditional dance or poetry writing (using brushes dipped in water only, illustrating the ephemeral and passing nature of life itself). Hopefully, the increased pollution which China's cities face will not erode the potential gains from these and other activities for older people. An alternative discourse on aging can point to ways in which the elderly can be *deproblematized* as a negative medical, economic, political and social category.

This must begin with appreciation of older people, first of all, as people rather than as a category (Powell 2006). Older people share, however, apart from their longevity, a wide and deep experience of life itself, and thus of life situations. In China, older people used to be venerated because they were, almost literally, the founts of wisdom, the holders of accumulated knowledge, far in advance of the younger members of the family and community(Chen and Powell 2012). Today, knowledge is far less likely to be oral, and far less dependent on accumulation by the individual. Instead, it is increasingly available at the touch of a button via an Internet search engine, even if there are some restrictions on web provision in the PRC. However, it can be suggested, there should still be a major role for the accumulated wisdom of older people's experiences as carriers of historical wisdom.

In China, there is a growing awareness of the need to have a sophisticated, multidimensional policy to respond to the needs of older people, but there is still a strong bio-medical emphasis on surveillance and control. It could be suggested that policy needs to be driven by the elderly themselves wherever possible. They should be encouraged to define and state their own needs and provided with support when this is required, but the overriding emphasis should be on providing support that fosters an active lifestyle and independent living wherever and whenever possible. This means encouraging the elderly to share their accumulated experience, to provide their oral histories and their views on the momentous changes that they, along with China itself, have lived through. Older people should be valued, and involved in wider society on terms that they themselves desire, recognizing that a wish for privacy and seclusion might be their preference.

Conclusion

Finally, it is worth noting that cases exist where narratives and micro-histories coexist and play a role in producing and strengthening social exclusion. The medical "gaze" refers here to discourses, languages, and ways of seeing that shape the understanding of aging into questions that center on, and increase the power of, the State, and restrict or de-legitimize other possibilities. A consequence is that areas of policy that may at first seem tangential to the medical project come to be reflected in its particular distorting mirror. The Chinese "Duomin"—a subcategory of a wider population officially catalogued as fallen people, beggars or ruined households—were seen as inferior and condemned to bear low status on account of a number of beliefs prevailing among mainstream society. The narrative concerns a creational myth that asserts that the Doumin were closely related to Chinese ethnic minorities like the She and Yao and that all these groups shared the belief in Pan-hu, a common dog ancestor. As to micro-histories, we run into different stories which state that the Doumin were either: (1) descendants of Song Dynasty traitors, deserters or prisoners; (2) remnants of antique non-Chinese ethnic groups; (3) foreigners who adopted the customs of Chinese lower social strata; and (4) descendants of domestic slaves. Yet in all cases, the Doumins excluded and outcaste status came about as a punishment society bestowed upon them. They were reduced to performing polluting occupations (ox head lanterns making, ironwork, barbers, caretakers, frog-catching, entertaining, among others) and limited to living in segregated quarters outside town. Furthermore, the Doumin were not allowed to study or take public office, nor serve as officers and were obliged to marry among themselves. This suggests that their social identity was a result of the legal status imposed on them and not the other way around. As Hansson (1996: 87) expresses it: "Once fallen people had been labeled as beggars, they had little choice but to conform to the behavior expected from people who had the social identity associated with their legal status." For older people, if they are regarded as an inferior category then their behavior will begin to mimic this categorization. "Dependent is as dependent does" is a major danger in the continuation of the dominance of the bio-medical model of aging.

A key point here is that the notion of the "bio-medical gaze" not only draws our attention to the ways that aging has become "medicalized" as a social issue in China; it also highlights the way in which older people are encouraged for as long as possible to "work on themselves" as active subjects. Thus, as Blaikie (1999) has pointed out, older citizens are encouraged to take greater personal responsibility for their health and for extending this period of their active aging. Those who are defined in relation to their health then discover themselves transformed into passive objects of medical power in China. How do we go beyond this in managing old age?

We could suggest macro-social practices have become translated into particular ways of growing old that not only shape what it is to age successfully, but are also adopted by older adults, modified to fit their own life circumstances and then fed back into wider narratives of aging well. Harry R. Moody (1998) coins this as the "Illderly" and "Wellderly," and managing aging experiences is about resistance to dominant discourses of bio-medicine. According to Frank (1998), the personal experience of illness is mediated by bio-medical procedures that shape and contribute to how the older people recognize their own process of ill health and recover. Katz (2000) notes that the maxim of "activity for its own sake" as a means of managing later life not only reflects wider social values concerning work and non-work; it also provides Personal means of control and acts as grounds for resistance. In addition, Phillipson (1998) argues that changes in westernized policies have occurred from seeing old age as a burden to seeing it as an opportunity to promote productive aging. This reflects an attempt to shape acceptable forms of aging while encouraging older adults to self-monitor their own success at conforming to the challenging paradigm of the hegemony of bio-medicine and its neglect of the agency of older people.

Chapter 4

A Foucauldian Analysis of Aging in China

Introduction

This chapter provides a theoretical critique and analysis of the development and consolidation of state power in China as it applies to aging. As shown in previous work (eg Li Yongping and Peng Xizhe, 2000; Powell and Cook, 2000; Powell and Cook 2010; Zhai Zhenwu, 2000), China's aging population is growing dramatically as a proportion of the total Chinese population, in part due to the success of the Communist Party of China (CPC) in delivering economic modernization to much of the population, but also due to knock-on effects of the Single Child Family Program, which has been in place, to a greater or lesser degree, since the 1970s, thus reducing the proportion of younger people within China (Murray, 1998). In seeking to deal with this increased proportion of elderly people, Chinese state policy can be seen as being essentially rational and fair-minded, seeking to introduce ways of reducing the fiscal burden of aging upon the state, and indeed upon those many families who have been markedly affected by the modernization process. This chapter, however, fundamentally questions the assumption that populational policies in the Chinese state are unbiased in their social practices with older people.

Indeed, narratives of social policy in Western culture have focused on old age with strong emphasis on the reform of social welfare (Biggs & Powell 2001). In the case of China, the process of political and economic reform was imposed in a top-down manner via "democratic centralism," supported by highly stretched demographic arguments (Powell & Cook 2000). These reforms purportedly offered the promise of greater choice and narratives of "people power" for both families and older people through the introduction of the market ethos (market socialism or "socialism with Chinese characteristics") into areas traditionally controlled, directly or indirectly (Powell & Cook 2000). The huge costs of welfare provision in recent decades by the Chinese government and have been subsidised by them via the lending programs of the state banking system.

The social rationale of such care provisos for older people has been at the center of debates within social gerontology in recent years on all sides of the Atlantic (Powell & Biggs 2000). A unique feature of the Chinese state in the 1990s was the systematic introduction of market-led principles throughout the public sector towards a plethora of modes of care provision. For example, family care constitutes a move away from direct state social care based on doomsday demographic projections coupled with powerful medical discourses of "decline" (Powell 2000).

In China, there has been, in the case of state language, a transition from "top down" health and social policies that provided care needs for dependent elderly populations through the quasi-welfare state, mapped out as the "'iron rice bowl'" of a job and support from the SOE for life, or the "5 guarantees" of the old commune system, to "'shelter, healthcare, food, clothing and burial'" (Cook 2001), to a State becoming more bottom up consumerism (Powell & Cook 2010). For example, one feature of the drive to speed up the development of tertiary industry instigated by the CPC in 1992 was to "gradually change the situation in which social services are provided by government offices, enterprises, and other institutions" (Yabuki, 1995: 300). The People's Republic of China introduced a law which came into force on October 1, 1996 on the "Rights and Interests of the Elderly," which explicitly states that:

Currently, social regulation and surveillance occur with an increasing pervasiveness of Western discourses of "social inclusion," which have been co-opted and absorbed into Chinese political and popular culture (Powell & Cook 2000). Hence, at the micro or grass roots level in China, family care is a technology put in place to challenge dependency by promoting "choice" of care services and instigating trust between the state and elderly people.

The Chinese political agenda has a number of key aims which have similarities with welfare systems in the United Kingdom, United States and Australasia (Powell & Cook, 2000): the control of financial resources, the improvement of services and promotion of choice, a reduction in public sector provision, and a focus on trust between state servants and older people. By 1992, for example, despite the situation of the elderly being regarded as important, government social welfare expenditure only constituted 3.5 percent of gross national income, and only 25 percent of the elderly were covered by the social security system (Du and Tu, 2000, op.cit.). Hence, to divert the resource burden from the state, the process of "choice" has become privatized and contingent on consumer sovereignty.

Simultaneously, the political, economic and social technology of state power has become a space for the surveillance of older people. It is argued here that the Chinese state is not of instigating narratives of "choice," but rather is a technology for collective control. Thus, there are two dimensions that are particularly important to the trajectory of this paper. Firstly, there is the use of a Foucauldian perspective to understand and explain the relationship between the Chinese state and elderly people. Secondly, there is the notion of "power" and its relevance to the consolidation of a narrative communicated by the Chinese state, which provides surveillance over a populational group: a Chinese "elderly population."

WHY FOUCAULT AS APPLIED TO CHINESE AGING?

Foucault's (1977) work has significance to the analysis of aging identity in two respects. First, his analysis of crime, deviance, punishment,discipline, medicine, and madness have relevance to the images and experiences of elderly people in China (Powell & Cook, 2000). A Foucauldian perspective can describe how subjects of knowledge, such as the stereotypical "elderly," are constructed through disciplinary technologies, for example, the notion of the expert and surveillance "gaze" (1973, 29). Secondly, Foucault (1977) makes it possible to analyze both the official discourses embodied in state policies, such as those of China, and those operating and implementing within society: families and their elderly relatives.

The diverse works of Foucault (1967, 1976 and 1977) have problematized issues of madness and illness, deviance and criminality, and sexuality although "'age" and "aging" were excluded from his work (Katz 1996; Powell & Biggs, 2000). These identity formations are defined as socially, politically and economically constructed "problems." In these social issues with aging aside, the work of Foucault has problematized the role of the "expert," social institutions that seem "empowering" but are historical constructions of discipline. The relevance to "age" and "aging" is the recognition that the power of the state can "define a certain pattern of 'normalization'" (Foucault 1977: 72). The diversity of surveillance practices is pivotal to Foucault's (1977) notion of "panoptic technology:"

> The carceral network, in its compact or disseminated forms, with its systems of insertion, distribution, surveillance, observation, has been the greatest support, in modern society, of the normalizing power (Foucault 1977: 304).

For Foucault (1977), "normalizing power" involves discourses and how these are asserted on the human body. Hence, the family plays a key role in such power relations, as they take responsibility for ensuring that individuals needs are regularly reviewed and that their own resources are effectively managed. We critically analyze Chinese policy developments and engage with a number of sites of the disciplinary web of surveillance and power and how these discursive formations impact Chinese older people.

Medical Power and the Construction and Problematization of Age

The definitions of centralized governmental assessments oriented around the care services needed for Chinese older people can be understood as a "system of ordered procedures for the production, regulation, distribution, circulation and operation of statements" (Foucault 1980: 133). All strategies that attempt to control Chinese older people involve the production and social construction of "true" knowledge. Historically, and before the prevalence of economic systems, bio-medicine played a key role in articulating "truths" about the social condition of older people (Katz 1996; Powell & Biggs 2000).

The relevance of this to Foucault's work is the way in which the "gaze" of truth constructs people as both subjects and objects of power and knowledge. In *The Birth of the Clinic*, Foucault illustrates how such a "gaze" opened up "a domain of clear visibility" (Foucault 1973: 105) for doctors, allowing them to construct an account of what was going on inside a patient, and to connect signs and symptoms with particular diseases. The space in which the gaze operated moved from the patient's home to the institution or the "hospital." This became the site for intensive surveillance, as well as the attainment of knowledge, the object of which was the body of patients. Both historically and contemporarily, the identities of elderly people and of old age have been constructed through expert discourses of "decay" and "deterioration," and the "gaze" helps to intensify regulation over older people in order to normalize and provide treatment for such notions (Foucault 1977; Katz 1996; Powell and Biggs 2000; Stott 1981). Medical discourse, under the guise of science, was part of a disciplinary project orientated to "create a model individual, conducting his life according to the precepts of health, and creating a medicalized society in order to bring conditions of life and conduct in line with requirements of health" (Cousins and Hussain 1984: 151).

The way in which bio-medicine has interacted with Chinese older people is a subtle aspect of control and power. This legitimizes the search within the individual for signs, for example, that s/he requires intense forms of surveillance and ultimately processes of medicalization. This permeates an intervention into Chinese aging lives because practices of surveillance befit elderly people because of the pathological discourse permeation of "its your age." In global culture, surveillance of older people enabled bio-medicine to show "concern" for their health and acquire knowledge about their condition. It, hence, constructs them as objects of power and knowledge:

> This form of power applies itself to immediate everyday life which categorises the individual, marks him by his own individuality, attaches him to his own identity, imposes a law of truth on him which he must recognise and which others have to recognise in him. It is a form of power which makes individuals subjects (Foucault 1982: 212).

In general, medical power took its place alongside state power in correcting, disciplining and normalizing "decaying" older people. Nevertheless, the Chinese state gaze at the beginning of the twenty-first century, has come to rival the medical gaze. The power of the state as a gerontological expert has supplemented medical power.

"Surveillance" and the Chinese State

Scientific dominance may have helped shape the construction of age identities, though it was not economical enough in its reach. Science has been bound up with "risk" (Beck 1984) and what Giddens (1991) calls the process of "reflexivity:" this manifests because of the loss of faith in the exercise of scientific power/knowledge. The focus on risk has led to a situation in which "science" has been slowly supplemented with financial discourses, and what we see, in relation to care provision in China, is an intensification towards family care models and consumerism. Hence, there is a pervasive move to a mixed economy of care, which has produced a new discourse aboutolder people in China as, "consumers" that has come to accompany and supplement medical discourses of old age, and impacts upon their treatment.

Indeed, the suspicion of scientific power/knowledge as manifested in "bio-medicine".

The perfect disciplinary apparatus, according to Foucault (1977: 173) "would make it possible for a single gaze to see everything perfectly." Foucault (1977) views the mechanism of panopticism as both efficient, since surveillance was everywhere and constant, and effective, because it was "discreet," functioning "permanently and in silence" (1977: 177). It also provides the scope for the supervision of those who were entrusted with the surveillance of others. In China, the process is indeed largely discreet and silent, for the monitoring and surveillance is more sophisticated than in previous decades, as the state has sought to distance itself from society, for instance via permitting a wider range of social and cultural forms than before, and encouraging consumerism as a distraction which serves to "atomize and privatize social life" (Blecher, 1997: 221).

The velvet globe contains an iron fist, which is revealed whenever the state feels itself threatened, as was seen in 1999 when the Falun Gong sect was banned following its earlier actions, which included a peaceful silent protest of 10,000 cult members outside the top leaders' compound at Zhongnanhai near Tiananmen, Beijing, in late April (Gittings, 1999). This, and other admittedly more extreme events, led to the cult being classed as "heretical," and a banning order was formalized at the 12th Session of the Standing Committee of the Ninth National People's Congress on October 30th (Beijing Review, 1999). One aspect which particularly worried the authorities was the involvement of quite senior CPC cadres in Falun Gong; another was the use of the Internet by the cult to organize demonstrations, and this subsequently led to greater restrictions on Internet use in the People's Republic in early 2000.

With regard to aging, the technique of "panopticism" was incorporated into state relationships so that older people could be observed by the Chinese state. Service provision for older people has elements of this kind of surveillance. Supervision is hierarchical in the sense that many older people are accompanied by state power which embraces monitoring, assessing and calculating older people. The Chinese state needs to keep informed of progress of older people in order to communicate this at committee meetings to establish resource allocation to service spending planning for its dependent populations. Surveillance of older people does not stop at this point, as a network of reciprocal power relationships has been created. This network 'holds' the whole together and traverses it in its entirety with effects of power that derive from one another: supervisors, perpetually supervised (Foucault 1977: 176-177).

The Probe of Surveillance

Foucault observes how the "norm" entered social science disciplines by "imposing new delimitations on them" (Foucault 1977: 184). While this standardized social science, it also had an individualizing effect "by making it possible to measure gaps, to determine levels, to fix specialities and to render the differences useful by fitting them to one another" (1977: 185). This also promoted the homogeneity of old age in China.

The identities of many older people are defined in relation to issues of abnormality and normality. The "cut off" point where an old individual is or is not deemed to be "frail" is in no sense clearly defined, and variations in levels of surveillance is of increasing concern for the Chinese state. In a climate of resource constraints due in part to the intensely competitive nature of globalization, distance from the norm has become valued amongst older people who do not conform to discourses of "slow" and "deterioration."

Foucault (1977) sees surveillance as a central technique that renders an individual an object of power/knowledge. In the surveillance relationship between the State and older people leading the opening for social services, the statement of an "aging body" is established in relation to normalized standards of rights and risks. Thus, older people will be probed for social, psychological and economic factors such as "frailty", "financial resources" and expected levels of "supervision" (Powell and Biggs 2000). There are indications, for example, that where care homes are provided, these are for the more active elderly, rather than those in greatest need. This probe of surveillance:

> indicates the appearance of a new modality of power in which each individual receives as his status his own individuality, and in which he is linked by his status to the features, the measurements, the gaps, the 'marks' that characterise him and makes him a 'case' (Foucault 1977: 192).

CONCLUSION

The impetus for this Foucauldian gerontological excursion derives from the view that older people bear the imprint of dominant modes of regulation both in terms of medical and state discourses and the decrease in resources to empower in contemporary China. Crucial questions have been raised as to the social relationships between the state and older people. As we transcend the fin-de-siecle, the metamorphosis of identities of "older people" into "consumers" in China is likely to fracture and consume older people still further, marginalizing the social and political context of care experiences and transforming discourses of "empowerment" into politically neutral and individually safe questions of satisfaction and dissatisfaction with the commodity or service offered by the Chinese state.

Chapter 5

AGING IDENTITY AND NARRATIVE IN CHINA

INTRODUCTION

To understand older people and the relationship to China, we must recognize that the historical meaning of old age changes in response to a wide variety of social, economic, political, cultural and inter-personal conditions. Social policies are both an attempt to shape and are themselves shaped by these meanings. In the United Kingdom, for example, much politicking has surrounded older people, including controversies over pensions, care and proposed legal reforms concerning employment. In Western societies, older people have been viewed in "burden" and "dependent" terms (Chen and Powell 2012). Conversely, pre-modern or traditional Chinese society placed elderly people on a pedestal (Cook, 2001). They were valued for their accumulated knowledge, their position within the extended family, and the sense of history and identity that they helped the family to develop (Murray, 1998). Respect for elderly people was an integral part of Confucian doctrine, especially for the family patriarch (Chen and Powell 2012).

Not only are people living longer, but they are doing so concurrently with the decrease in births associated with the People's Republic of China (henceforth PRC) Single Child Family Program. Du and Tu (2000) identify four "unique characteristics" of China's population aging:

Unprecedented speed: the proportion of the elderly is growing faster than Japan, the country previously recognized as having the fastest rate, and much faster than nations in Western Europe for example.

Early arrival of an aging population: before modernization has fully taken place, with its welfare implications. "It is certain that China will face a severely aged population before it has sufficient time and resources to establish an adequate social security and service system for the elderly" (ibid: 79).

Fluctuations in the total dependency ratio: Chinese estimates are that the country will reach a higher "dependent burden" earlier in the twenty-first century than was previously forecast.

Strong influence of the government's fertility policy and its implementation on the aging process: the Single Child Family Program means fewer children being born, but with more elderly people a conflict arises between the objectives to limit population increase and yet maintain a balanced age structure (Chen and Powell 2011).

The combination of such factors means that the increased number of the elderly is giving rise to serious concerns among Chinese policy makers. The next section looks at how politics impinge on dominant construction of old age in China.

Politics, Power and Representations of Old Age in the Chinese Communist Party

For the Chinese Communist Party (CCP) which rules China, the view of the elderly has been highly variable, and sometimes contradictory. For much of the time the Party has viewed the elderly essentially as dependents, to be looked after by work unit or family as the case may be, and yet, within the Party hierarchy, the elderly assumed a major role, either within its formal structures such as the Politburo, or when ostensibly retired from these organizations informally via more shadowy "advisory" bodies which retain great power. The CCP itself has a tradition of elderly active within its power structures, and its great leaders, Mao Zedong, Zhou Enlai and Deng Xiaoping, worked to a very great age, into their eighties. Two examples illustrate this point.

Firstly, there is Mao's activities during the mid-1960s. Born in 1893 he was by then in semi-retirement, partly shunted aside by the CCP after the failures of the Great Leap Forward. In 1965 he orchestrated a spectacular propaganda coup by swimming in the Yangtze River at the venerable age of 72, accompanied by photographers in motor launches. Where he swam, off Wuhan, the river is nearly two miles wide, and beset by difficult currents. Mao, however, was always a strong swimmer. Moreover, provided the swimmer follows the current downstream, at an angle to the river, and swims in the warm summer waters, great distance can be achieved. The impact on China, and indeed overseas opinion, was startling. For home consumption, "this exercise at such a place was no doubt partly designed to refute the fears and superstitions of the people who still dreaded the 'River Dragon,' which devours swimmers" (Fitzgerald, 1976: 138). Mao built on this success to launch the Great Proletarian Cultural Revolution the following year, having reconfirmed his cult status.

In a less dramatic, but no less important, vein was the role of Deng Xiaoping and others of the "eight elders" during Tiananmen in 1989. Born in 1904, Deng was thus 85 at this time, and some of the other elders were even older. They came together to express their concerns over what they viewed as too soft a response by the Politburo Standing Committee to the ongoing student protest in the square. They still had power, and used it firstly on May 18th to meet with the Standing Committee (minus Zhao Ziyang, then General Secretary of the CCP and a noted reformer, known to be sympathetic to many of the views held by the students) and the leaders of the key Central Military Commission to order that Beijing be put under martial law. Zhao Ziyang was ousted, and on May 21st "Deng Xiaoping convened the Party elders to take charge since the younger generation of leaders seemed unable to manage" (Nathan and Link, 2001: 223). They agreed on Jiang Zemin, the current leader of the PRC, as the replacement for Zhao Ziyang at a meeting on May 27th. Finally, on June 2nd, the fateful decision was taken to clear the square by force, and on June 4, 1989, the terrible die was cast at Tiananmen, despite Deng Xiaoping's instructions to avoid bloodshed in the square itself. Deng Xiaoping's image in the West as a small "cuddly uncle" who wore tengallon hats during his visits to the U.S.A. and was behind the reform period in China, was changed completely for his part in Tiananmen. However he revived his tainted reputation as far as the West was concerned, or at least Western businessmen, via his famous South China tour in 1992 at an even more advanced age (Cook and Murray, 2001). During this tour, allegedly under armed guard, Deng courageously backed further opening up in China, and this gave the green light to a massive foreign investment in the country, to a "China Fever" which led to Deng Xiaoping receiving *Time*'s "Man of the Year" accolade in 1992. By then he was 87, and remained in remarkably rude health, given that he was well-known as a chain smoker right up to his death at the age of 93 in February 1997.

THE AGING POPULATION IN CHINA

Traditionally, the elderly may have been "placed on a pedestal" as noted previously, but the lack of any welfare system in traditional Chinese peasant society meant that many elderly had to keep farming the land, regardless of their age. Image 1, taken from a book first published in 1927, shows an aged Chinese farmer in his warm winter garb. He uses a staff, his beard is white and his forehead is etched with lines, but he stands erect and still maintains an air of vigor. Even after more than 50 years of communism, the elderly in the countryside are, "generally physically stronger than their counterparts in the cities and accustomed to doing physical work, [and] many continue to live on their own earnings by doing what they can" (Yu, 1987: 210). Official data in the 1990s show that 26 percent of old people in rural areas still depend on their own labor earnings compared to only 7 percent in towns and cities (Sun 1996). Therefore, the tradition of the active elderly in rural areas continues. However, less arduous forms of recreation abound as well. In Beijing, for example, there is an army veterans' chorus. Another group of veterans has just published a collection of poems. Clubs, parks, activity rooms and homes for the aged are being established in many cities.

Other retirees are active in neighborhood committees, giving a hand with such civic duties as helping children with educational activities, mediating disputes, helping with traffic control, doing welfare work, and serving the neighborhood in various ways. The elderly in the countryside are also doing what they can for their homes and community, such as offering technical advice based on their long years of farming experience (Yu, 1987: 212-13).

Within, the People's Republic of China there are genuine concerns to improve the well-being of the elderly, as shown in the latest five-year plan, for example, as well as a range of recent measures to improve the profile of the elderly and the attention paid to them (Guo, 2001; Tang 2001b; Zeng 2001). The increased longevity points to the progress already made within the country. We could argue that, as far as possible, policies should build on those introduced in the 1980s to encourage physical and gentler exercise of the type illustrated above by Yu. There should also be a renewal of the ancient system of respect for the elderly, albeit without the fear or deference which was often found in traditional society. To value the elderly, to involve them wherever possible, and to view them as a resource rather than as a problem would seem to us the way forward, in China and elsewhere. Hence, we are also sensitized to the concept of living with multiple narratives that impinges on viewing old age in many dimensions.

In summary, we have argued that future developments in policy analysis in China will have to take both tacit and explicit themes in populational policy into account as they relate to elderly people. They will also have to more closely examine the relationship between personal story-making and formal public policy discourses in China (Chen and Powell 2012).

Policies provide narrative templates within which certain categories of persons or groups are encouraged to live out their lives. However, this legitimized performance may differ significantly from an individual's or group's everyday experience of that same role, function, or social space, leading to conflict between different levels of narrative.

Chapter 6

THE STATE, TRUST AND AGING IN CHINA

INTRODUCTION

Like so many other fundamental, taken-for-granted concepts of everyday life, "trust" is scarcely analyzed and rarely understood (Powell and Owen, 2005). Although trust is a commonly used word, most people in almost every social relationship would probably be "hard-pressed" to provide a definition of trust as the concept is used in different ways and to refer to different social, political, economic and cultural contexts. Similarly, sociological and other social-scientific discussions of trust are characterized by imprecision and ambiguity, which, although tolerable in everyday conversation, is unacceptable if "trust" is to be employed as a concept with some theoretical utility. Trust receives a great deal of pubic exposure grounded in the assumption that the level of trust placed by the public in particular offices, institutions or systems is critical to its continuing authority. This chapter develops some ideas about the concept of trust and its potential application to the theoretical study of aging and China. Trust, either personal or impersonal (Misztal 1996), can be viewed as fundamental to interpersonal relationships (Brownlie and Howson 2005), to the working of social systems and state institutions (Luhmann 1979, Giddens 1990), and to social cohesion (Misztal 1996, Putman 1993), all linked to the public world of modernity. It is the relationship to the Chinese state and older people that interest us. Indeed, we are writing this chapter in the couple of years following the British General Election where the central plank of the opposition's challenge to the Blair government was that Blair had lost the "trust" of the British people because of the Iraq War. The moral challenge implied by this criticism was sufficient for many commentators to conclude that despite the fact that he had won a third General Election, as a politician, Prime Minister Tony Blair was seriously if not mortally wounded by loss of trust. What is clear from this and other examples is that trust provides a pivot on which fortunes can flourish or perish. Trust is a dynamic category and a contested quality, giving rise to a "politics of trust" (Phillipson and Powell, 2004).

In this chapter, we consider the question of trust and how different conceptions of trust provide epistemic insights into the conditions upon which trust operates in China. For without trust, state activities in China reliant on co-operation between individuals and communities with future orientated expectations have no satisfactory basis on which they might be established.

The chapter is divided into three sections. The first considers some of the ways in which trust is conceptualized. Trust is worthy of the attention of social scientists because trust relates to such topical and widely debated sociological issues as consumerism (and hence to debates on post-modernity) and knowledge/communication. An improved understanding of the concept of trust gives a deeper theoretical understanding of these issues.

We explore the use of the concept within various social scientific fields, and compare it to the sociological literature on trust. It outlines some requirements for a specifically sociological conception of trust, and emphasizes the need to distinguish between different levels and dimensions of trust. Considerable clarification and refinement of this kind is required if 'trust" is to become a truly useful theoretical tool within the social sciences. The second part looks at the history of China and aging and problematizes whether trust relations have been pertient to describe social relations between the state and Chinese families and older people.

Finally, the paper looks at contemporary China and assesses the extent to which trust relations can be built upon through use of Foucault's post-structuralist notion of techniques of self.

Understood in a post-structuralist context, trust in its micro-political terms and conceived as impacting on individual identity and agency at a number of levels: intrapersonal, personal, interpersonal, systems or organisational levels and the socio-political (Molling, 2001); this relationship stands at the interface of competing pressures working to produce the increasing complexity of social life (Powell, 2005; Chen and Powell 2012) as well as in China (Cook and Powell, 2005; Powell and Cook, 2006). "Trust" is inextricably linked with uncertainty and complexity, while professional power rests on the specialist knowledge claimed by the range of governmental experts and technologists that inhabit the spaces through which Chinese life is governed and complexity managed. Spaces are at once both hidden and visible, which provide opportunities across the social landscape for the agency of individuals to be exercised and worked on, producing the self-managing consumer citizen central to Chinese government, conceptually defined as "governmentality" (Powell and Cook, 2001). In this context the strategies of trust become linked with rival programs that come armed with a range of technologies charged with competing and contested truth claims (Powell, 2005). As a consequence, contradictory positions are provided where selfish desire and selfless obligation are placed together sharing the same space, thus adding to the potential for anxiety and provoking searches for *ontological security* in China amongst older people and aging populations (Cook and Powell, 2001).

It is in these spaces that expert knowledge works upon the dual project of managing both its conduct and the conduct of others (Foucault, 1991). In managing state systems, expertise deploying a range of systems of mistrust are designed to both reassure the population of the integrity of the system and the authority of the expertise embedded there (Reddy, 1996). At the same time this expertise claims the right to accredit and provide the necessary symbols of authority of state power (nationalism CCCP) to control populations through social policy and increasing reliance on consumerism and market forces (Chen and Powell 2012). Before we interrogate the notion of trust and consider its relevance in historical China in social relations, we briefly dissect its conceptual and experiential influence in social sciences.

WHAT IS TRUST?

There are increasing attempts to conceptualize the notion of "trust" in social science as a pivotal dimension of late modernity. However, the early statement that "social science research on trust has produced a good deal of conceptual confusion regarding the meaning of trust and its place in social life" (Lewis and Weigert 1985 quoted in Powell, 2005, 44) seems to be still valid, especially as applied to aging studies. Trust is on the one hand incompatible with complete ignorance of the possibility and probability of future events, and on the other hand with emphatic belief when the anticipation of disappointment is excluded.

Someone who trusts has an expectation directed to an event. The expectations are based on the ground of incomplete knowledge about the probability and incomplete control about the occurrence of the event. Trust is of relevance for action and has consequences for the trusting agent if trust is confirmed or disappointed (Powell, 2005).

Up to now there have been few attempts to work out a systematic scheme of different forms of trust in between older people and individuals, health institutions or policies that impinge on their identity performance (Powell and Cook, 2003). Social trust tends to be high among older people who believe that their public safety is high (Wahidin and Powell, 2001). Since the erosion of public trust in institutions like the government and the media (Chen and Powell 2012), trust attracts more and more attention in social sciences.

Trust seems to be something that is produced individually by experience over time and cannot be immediately and purposely produced by organizations or state governments without dialogical interaction with older people on issues in Asia affecting their lifestyles and life-chances, such as care, pensions, employment and political representation (Walker and Naeghele, 2000). Now, we move to problematize trust and situate it within the context of historical China.

TRUST AND CHINA: AN HISTORIOGRAPHY

Historically, who did the Chinese trust? In occidental modernity, an answer to a question such as this might well begin with the self, before moving outwards to the family, community or nation. In China, however, the self was very much subjugate to the wider society of family, clan, or the Chinese state. Within the family, rights were minimal, except for those of the patriarch, up to a point also the eldest son, and, to an extent and commensurate with age and motherhood, the elderly mother. Family members were subordinate to the family itself, an entity that spanned the generations and included the dead ancestors in one direction and the unborn descendants in the other.

The ancestors could turn against living family members should they fail to act for the good of the family, bringing curses and disasters to their own descendants if necessary. The regular Confucian rites and rituals of ancestor worship ensured that, most of the time, the forebears were kept "on side", but woe betide the family member who neglected their duties in this regard.

> From the beginning of Chinese civilization, members of the same clan had acknowledged and worshipped the authority of their deceased ancestors; for, dead though they were, their powers were thought to be no less overawing than those of the contemporary leader who was their descendant (Loewe, 1973, 109)

There was also power manifest in the spirits of the heavens and the earth. "The river dragon has come" was the classic cry when the river burst its banks, as happened so regularly in China's densely populated delta areas, and although the phrase had a literal sense in the snakes and lizards that would be propelled by the raging torrent, there was also the spiritual dimension betokening the release of the great dragons that inhabited China.

Within this world in which floods on the one hand and famine on the other played such a regular and disastrous role, trust would come from Confucian ritual or Daoist worship, membership of family, clan, village and possibly secret societies (groups with "fanciful names like the Triads, the Yellow Turbans, the White Lotus, or the Fists of Righteous Harmony" (Dreyer, 1996, 31)), or via the Mandate of Heaven through officials and gentry to the Emperor himself.

This was the world of feudalism, one of the two great mountains that Mao Zedong identified as bearing down on the Chinese people, with the other being imperialism. Together with the Chinese masses, the Chinese Communist Party (CCP) would smash these mountains and liberate the people from these heavy burdens. The communist revolution did indeed provide liberation, and many in the new China began to trust the CCP rather than the ancestors, family patriarch or village head.

Party cadres for instance were required to be people of great probity, who were sent "to the villages" where they "were expected to participate regularly in production alongside the peasants, live in similar circumstances with them, and in general share their experiences" (Blecher, 1997, 27). Themselves raised in the authoritarian traditions of China, this was not always easy for these cadres, who were subject to "rectification campaigns" to ensure that they worked with, rather than on, the masses.

Similarly, and crucially, People's Liberation Army (PLA) members forsook the traditional means of Chinese soldiers to take whatsoever they wanted by force; instead purchasing what they required and helping the people rather than exploiting them. By such means and others, for many in China trust grew in the CCP, contrasting with mistrust in the nationalists and the Guomindang, and the revolution was eventually achieved.

Although struggling against the "nationalists" Mao nonetheless believed in a strong China, therefore his leftism was itself tempered by nationalism. With the CCP becoming the leadership of the People's Republic of China this has meant that governance and party policy have become intertwined and interwoven in an increasingly complex way. Mao and his successors have been concerned with ensuring that the Party remains strong, but also that China remains strong. Nationalism has therefore remained an important factor in China's politics, and for some, therefore, trust is expressed in "China" rather than the Chinese Communist Party.

Trust has grown in the CCP, the government, the nation or all three taken together. In recent years, however, even trust in these great edifices has at times been called into doubt, partly as a result of the great transformation working through modern Chinese society. And so:

> the leadership [of the CCP] has been forced to face the reality that in many parts of rural China, the Party's word is no longer law. According to a 'party source' quoted by the South China Morning Post, a survey of 10 provinces showed rural party cells had lost legitimacy and power. 'The survey finds real power in the villages resides with heads of clans or even leaders of underground churches and cults,' the source said. 'Jiang [then leader Jiang Zemin] was alarmed on hearing that clan and cult leaders in relatively remote hamlets can often take the law into their own hands'. By contrast, party committees in villages, which are supposed to lay down the rules, fail to command the respect of the people (South China Morning Post, 9-10-1998) (Cook and Murray, 2001, op.cit., 248).

Trust and Aging in Contemporary China

The challenges faced by the state over the last twenty-five years or so, such as the increasing health costs of an aging population (Rose 1999, DoH 2005), have been matched by rapid social change. One effect of this has been the fragmentation of welfare away from a monolithic state organization to one co-ordinated and financed by the state but disciplined by market mechanisms such as commissioning and competitive tendering (Clarke and Newman 1997, Lewis and Gillam 2003). Another effect has been the politicization of trust. Distrust and protest has become a feature of life in China today. In 2005, official data recorded 70,000 protests, 50,000 of these concerning environmental issues, across the country. Trust in the

Party is breaking down in many areas. At the time of writing, the authorities have just closed an online survey that, according to unofficial blogs, claims to have shown that of 10,000 respondents who were asked if they would prefer a different nationality if they were born again, 64% said yes they would, mainly because "Chinese citizens lacked human dignity" (Watts, 2006). Of those people who wished to be born again as Chinese, "love of the country" was given by 19% of these respondents.

As for elderly people in China, state policies have varied considerably since the establishment of the PRC. In the Maoist era there was great concern to reduce the authority of family elders, given that the latter were so closely associated with the previous feudal era. "The campaign against the aged is not so much an attempt to break down family authority as an effort to remould citizens' attitudes" (Liu, 1973: 688). The Great Proletarian Cultural Revolution (GPCR) lasted from 1966-1976, (although it peaked around 1970, after which the young Red Guards were reined in via deployment of the PLA) and witnessed the vulnerability of the elderly to being denounced as bourgeois reactionaries by the manipulated young. Trust in the state among the elderly must have been seriously eroded during this period, although this would have been offset in part, and especially in rural areas, via health and welfare support via the "5 guarantees" within the commune system. The subsequent reform period under Deng Xiaoping and his successors have brought different contradictions for the Chinese elderly. The state, via the CCP, is no longer obviously aggressive towards the elderly, but marketization policies mean that trust too has become a commodity for exchange (Dasgupta 1988). Demanding new forms of governance and producing a paradox, consumer autonomy for older people released from direct management by the state is matched by ever more-complex forms of surveillance and control of their behavior, both as individuals and as aging populations (Powell and Cook, 2005).

One feature of the established order in the last quarter of the last century in China was one where the institutionalized interests of state professionals were considered to stand in opposition to both the views of particular sections of the state and the newly produced subject position of "people power" (Clarke and Newman 1997). Since the 1980s, claims of a decline in the authority of the state professions accompanied this process, replaced by consumer models of identity performance. Public perceptions of failures of professional self-regulation articulate as institutionalized self-interest (Davies 2000), paralleled by the increasing power, or resistance by state professionals.

The reciprocal relationship between the state and the personal lives of older Chinese citizens is central to the analysis of the role and performance of public services. In a mutually constitutive process, the social experience and identities of individual citizens are produced, in part, through engagement with public services, which are then affected by the actions of those citizens (Molling, 2001). The fact that experiences of Chinese state services impact on different spheres of older people's lives implies that the exploration of trust also has to explore these different domains, but in an integrated multi-disciplinary way that enables comparison between the different criteria upon which trust is established, maintained or lost (Reddy, 1996). Such an approach to trust is aided by the existence of similar concerns across domains. These include: trust as future orientated, trust that occurs without the guarantee of reciprocity, trust that requires the placing of expectations with the agency of others, trust that works to reduce complexity and anxiety, and trust that involves risk and uncertainty. At the same time the observation that mistrust operates as the functional equivalent to trust provides a means of considering the complex interplay between expectations and sanctions (Luhmann 1979).

Trust is a complex idea which can be explored theoretically and empirically on different levels: politically in relation to social capital and social norms; sociologically in relation to abstract systems, complexity and risk; and inter-personally in relation to characteristics of trustworthiness such as competence. Trust can be conceived as generalized, e.g., through the level of trust based exchanges between older members of a Chinese community, or as particular, as in personal relationships (Luhman, 1989).

Conceptually there are tensions but also interesting theoretical possibilities between late modern and post-modern conceptions of society. Both identify the fragmentation of traditional forms of authority and expertise and acknowledge the increasing complexity this produces through the availability of multiple sources of information and different lifestyle choices. This uncertainty gives rise to an increasing reliance on trust in the agency of others (Seligman 1997). Late [high] modern conceptions of trust tend to point to the failure of rational choice theories to account for human behavior as evidence for the existence of a range of social norms that promote altruistic behaviors, obligation and responsibility (Giddens, 1991).

Post-structuralists, in particular governmentality theorists, have discussed risk and uncertainty at length (Rose 1993), but leave the discussion of "trust" to an observation that the trust traditionally placed in authority figures has been replaced by audit culture (Powell, 2001). Concerns about social norms could be reframed within a post-structuralist lens by locating the debate about trust with those relating to Foucault's notion of "technologies of the self" (Foucault, 1988).

As stated earlier, trust and responsiveness are assumed to be the issues of central concern with state transparency providing supporting technologies through which trust is promoted and maintained. The discussion will now turn to explore the relationship between trust, transparency and responsiveness. For the purpose of this section Luhmann's (1993) definition of trust as "managing expectations and reducing complexity" is assumed.

In considering the performance of the state in China, a balance of consumerist "choice" and participatory "voice" is essential to the quality and performance of public policy as well as reinforcement of state power. Responsiveness becomes a blend of choice and voice at both individual and organizational levels, with the proposition that older consumers will participate in the setting of family groups sizes targets (legitimized as populational control process) while individual older consumers will be able to modify services to meet individual needs(Chen and Powell 2012).

The Chinese government position is underpinned by a model of human behavior that assumes individuals will balance their own needs with an element of social responsibility, which also reflects a good deal of Chinese governmental discourse around encouraging older people into paid work, as highlighted in the previous chapter regarding policy narratives of aging (Cook and Powell, 2003).

If we take the sentiments expressed in populational policies in China to be an expression of the discourses circulating through social policy and link this with the analysis of Foucault's post-structuralist concept of "governmentality," we can see the possible conditions in which self-subjectification can be managed. The deployment of consumerist discourses of citizenship enable the population to be managed. The management of older people who require intensive health care has shifted from large institutions, to management through the community (Rose 1996). However, the discourse of normalization which underpinned the move from institutions has been transformed into a discourse of citizenship, with many vulnerable older people now managed in the community, which remain supervised by unaccountable social workers/ care managers in China (Powell and Cook, 2000; Powell and Cook 2010).

The task of the state is to encourage older people in China to move along a continuum towards self-management while they anticipate and manage the risks involved (Chen and Powell 2012). These discourses of citizenship provide a number of reference points, e.g., work and obligation to a particular community, but the partial and fragmented way these discourses penetrate both policy and everyday life for older people means that a number of different, often contradictory positions are established. The differences between the different models of support, residential care and supported living are evidence of this uneven process in China.

Governmentality, Trust and Self-Actualization

Despite the fragmented nature of the outcomes for older people, we can consider the different outcomes in relation to the ethic of the self central to governmentality (Chen and Powell 2012). This ethic, deployed through the discourses of citizenship, works to construct older people as useful while also identifying those who are greater risk. The latter experience further segregation and surveillance by state professionals with more coercive technologies. As noted earlier, this ethic of the self is composed of four dimensions: ethical substance, mode of subjection, self forming activity, and telos or end product. It concerns the way aging bodies are made useful, productive and self-managing. These dimensions will now be considered in relation to choices and opportunities produced for older people in China.

The first model, the *ethical substance*, is that part of the self that is to be worked and subjected to ethical judgement. In this context we can consider the identity formed and the feelings of responsibility and obligation being produced. The identities of citizen-tenant, of worker, as consumer in the markert, as member of the Chinese community, are suggestive of a new identity for Chinese older people. These identities are formed in opposition to previous identities of dependence. At the same time, feelings of responsibility are created as older individuals become accountable for their choices and obligation.

The second model is the *mode of subjection* and relates to the way in which the Chinese individual recognizes themselves in accordance with particular rules and norms and puts these into practice. The recognition of oneself as citizen-tenant, worker, consumer, and member of a Chinese community requires the older person to actively engage in these processes and, through this engagement, to demonstrate their compliance with the rules and norms. There are examples of older individuals engaging in work and exercising consumer choice (Du and Tu, 1999). In relation to community based voluntary work, the two themes of work and affiliation to a particular community are brought together clearly paralleling the consumerist view of citizenship that is expressed by Chinese policy on health and social policy for older people (Walker, 2005).

The third element is the *self forming activity* or ethical work required to transform and develop the individual as an ethical subject. This relates to the particular practices individuals engage in to maintain their identity. In relation to governmentality, Rose and Miller (1992) identify a range of techniques where individuals work upon themselves to modify their behaviors, improve their knowledge and develop skills linked to their Chinese identity and modes of subjection. Many of these activities relate to reflective and confessional practices. However, in relation to older people we might identify practices that sustain individual self-discipline, i.e., appearance, maintenance of personal space, and relationships with others. In the marginalized spaces that older people occupy, these self-forming activities are mediated, encouraged and supported by state workers (Powell and Biggs, 2000)

The final model dimension, *telos*, relates to the aim governmentality: the production of the useful, productive and ethically self managing individual; the role of services and State social workers is to encourage and support people towards this goal (Powell and Cook, 2003).

The implication of these four dimensions of governmentality is that the state's role as facilitator contains profound interpersonal power/knowledge relations in terms of who controls and allows access to resources, which simultaneously intereact with the economic, social, and cultural capital of the professional worker and the older person within particular Chinese communities.

CONCLUSION

This chapter has explored the notion of trust in relation to older people in China and the assumption that policy penetrates into the lives of people in partial, fragmented and locally specific ways. The analysis of governmentality provides a rich picture for theorizing. Rather than evaluating the adequacy of particular discourses, governmentality identifies strategies that work to make individuals productive and self-managing. First, there are marginalized spaces were older people are maintained and subjected to techniques of surveillance by professional social workers (Powell and Cook, 2001; Cook and Powell, 2010). Second, the different discourses of citizenship, while producing contradictory positions for older people, do nevertheless provide positions of independence to be had when less than half a century ago no such positions were advocated by Chinese government (Chen and Powell 2012). In this sense these discourses are productive and the role of professionals is to move people along the continuum towards governmentality through trust relations. The analysis of governmentality enables the identification of a range of techniques that work to make older people exercise self-government (Powell, 2001) outside of traditional images of state power in China.

Chapter 7

BEYOND CHINA? AGING IN ASIA

This book has so far focused on the issue of China and the social and theoretical implications for understanding aging. This concluding chapter attempts to "go beyond" China and focus comparative analysis with other countries in Asia. Asia itself has the fastest increase in the aging population in the world.

The combination of such factors means that the increased aging population is giving rise to serious concerns among Chinese policy makers. Kim and Lee (2007) claim the growing elderly population is beginning to exert pressure on the East Asian countries economies. Three decades ago, major industrialized countries have begun to grapple with the similar problem. With increasing drop in fertility rates, more East Asian economies such as Japan, Hong Kong, South Korea, Singapore and Taiwan are expected to turn into "super-aging societies" by 2025 (Kim and Lee 2007). However, the magnitude of the future impact depends on the (in)ability of individual economies to resolve the demographic changes problem through increased privatisation, pension reforms, a migration on more productive countries and extension of retirement age. Like western countries, Asia will ultimately have to tackle issues related to pension reform and the provision of long term health care services (Cook and Powell, 2007).

For Japan, the basic statistical reality of its demographic profile is escalating. Already, 17 of every 100 of its people are over 65, and this ratio will near 30 in 15 years. From 2005 to 2012, Japan's workforce is projected to shrink by around 1% each year - a pace that will accelerate after that. Economists fear that, besides blowing an even bigger hole in Japan's underfunded pension system (Cook and Powell, 2007), the decline of workers and young families will make it harder for Japan to generate new wealth.

The future challenge of providing for the elderly is especially urgent in the world's two biggest nations - India and China. Only 11% of Indians have pensions, and they tend to be civil servants and the affluent. With a young population and relatively big families, many of the elderly population still count on their children for support. This is not the case in China. By 2030, there will be only two working-age people to support every retiree. Yet only 20% of workers have government- or company-funded pensions or medical coverage (Chen and Powell 2011). However, as a counterbalance to such a gloomy perspective, 'Chindia' (China and India taken together) is currently accumulating vast wealth as a result of global change, wealth that could potentially be redirected for the support of their elderly populations. But why has global aging been an unstoppable force to restrain the potential and exponential growth of such economies to fullest potential which could be way beyond the projected 9% growth for China (Chen and Powell 2012).

The Consequences of Aging in Asia

While global aging represents a triumph of medical, social, and economic advances, it also presents tremendous challenges for many regions of the world and Asia is no different. Population aging strains social insurance and pension systems and challenges existing models of social support traditionally given by family structures (Bengston and Lowenstein 2004). It affects economic growth, trade, migration, disease patterns and prevalence, and fundamental assumptions about growing older. Global aging will have dramatic effects on local, regional, and global economies. Chris Phillipson (1998) has argued that the rise of globalization exerts unequal and highly stratified effects on the lives of older people in different nation states (Phillipson 1998; Estes 2001). In the developed world, the magnitude and absolute size of expenditure on programs for older people has made these the first to be targeted with financial cuts. In less developed countries, older people (women especially) have been amongst those most affected by the privatization of health care, and the burden of debt repayments to the World Bank and the IMF. Additionally, globalization as a process that stimulates population movement and migration may also produce changes that disrupt the lives of older people (Chen and Powell 2012). And one must not forget either that they may comprise up to one-third of refugees in conflict and emergency situations - a figure which was estimated at over 53 million older people worldwide in 2000.

Changes in the age structures of societies also have consequences for total levels of labor force participation in society, because the likelihood that an individual will be in the labor force varies systematically by age (Phillipson, 1998). Labor itself is viewed as less mobile than capital, although migration could offset partially the effects of population aging. Currently, 22 percent of physicians and 12 percent of nurses in the United States are foreign born, representing primarily African countries, the Caribbean, and Southeast Asia (OECD 2007). The foreign-born workforce also is growing in most OECD countries. Over the next 10 years, the European experience will be particularly instructive in terms of the interplay of aging and migration (OECD 2007). It is also because the future is already dawning that global trends impact on state power. In South Korea and Japan, which have strong cultural aversions to immigration, small factories, construction companies, and health clinics are relying more on 'temporary' workers from the Philippines, Bangladesh, and Vietnam (OECD 2007). In China, state industries are struggling over how to lay off unneeded middle-age workers when there is no social safety net to support them (Cook and Powell, 2007). What really has pushed aging to the top of the global agenda, though, is increasing fiscal gaps (in part, due to the "global credit crunch") in the U.S., Europe, Japan, and elsewhere that could worsen as populations reach retirement age. While U.S. Social Security is projected to remain solvent until at least 2042, the picture is more acute in Europe. Unlike the U.S., where most citizens also have private savings plans, in much of Europe up to 90% of workers rely almost entirely on public pensions (Walker and Naeghele 2000). Austria guarantees 93% of pay at retirement, for example, and Spain offers 94.7%. Concurrently, global population aging is projected to lead to lower proportions of the population in the labor force in highly industrialized nations, threatening both productivity and the ability to support an aging population (Chen and Powell 2012). It is possible for the elements of production—labor and capital—to flow across national boundaries and mitigate the impact of population aging (Phillipson 1998). Studies predict that, in the near term, capital accumulation will flow from Europe and North America to emerging markets in Asia and Latin America , where the population is younger and supplies of capital relatively low. In another 20 years, when the "baby boom" generation in the West has mostly retired, the consequence is that capital will likely flow in the opposite direction (May and Powell, 2007).

It is interesting that the World Bank (1994) foresees growing 'threats' to international stability with the consequence of pitting different demographic-economic regions against one another (Phillipson, 1998). The United Nations (2002) view the relationship between aging populations and labor force participation with panic recognizes important policy challenges, including the need to reverse recent trends toward decreasing labor force participation of workers in late middle and old age despite mandatory retirement in certain western countries such as the UK (Powell, 2005). Social welfare provisions and private-sector pension policies influencing retirement income have a major impact on retirement timing. Hence, a major concern for organizations such as United Nations and World Bank centers on the number of such 'dependent' older people in all developing societies. Furthermore, nation states with extensive social programs targeted to the older population—principally health care and income support programs—find the costs of these programs escalating as the number of eligible recipients grows and the duration of eligibility lengthens due to global pressures (Bengtson and Lowenstein 2003). Further, few countries have fully funded programs; most countries fund these programs on a pay-as-you-go basis or finance them using general revenue streams. Governments may be limited in how much they can reshape social insurance programs by raising the age of eligibility, increasing contribution rates, and reducing benefits. Consequently, shortfalls may need to be financed using general revenues. Projections of government expenditures in the United States and other OECD countries show increases in the share of gross domestic product devoted to social entitlements for older populations. In some cases, this share more than doubles as a result of population aging (OECD 2007). Different countries' age groups have different levels of pace of growth (Phillipson, 1998; Estes, Biggs and Phillipson, 2003).

The life-cycle theory of consumption is that family households accumulate wealth during working years to maintain consumption in retirement (Gilleard and Higgs 2001). The total of a country's individual life-cycle savings profiles determines whether households in that country are net savers or no savers at any point in time. A country with a high proportion of workers will tend to be dominated by savers, placing downward pressure on the rate of return to capital in that economy. Nation states with older populations will be tapping their savings and driving rates of return higher because of the scarcity of capital (Gilleard and Higgs 2001). This impacts on pensions. Most of Europe's state-funded pension systems encourage early retirement. Now, 85.5% of adults in France retire from employment by age 60, and only 1.3% engages in employment beyond aged 65. In Italy, 62% of adults retire from full-time work by the age of 55. That compares with 47% of people who earn wages or salaries until they are 65 in the U.S. and 55% in Japan (Estes 2001).

Individual and family resources are important too. These typically include public and private pensions, financial assets, and property. Pensions and elder-care costs will increase from 14% of capitalist nations' gross domestic product to 18% by 2050 (Walker and Naeghele 2000). The relative importance of these resources varies across countries. For example, a groundbreaking study revealed that only 3% of Spanish households with at least one member age 50 or older own stocks (shares), compared to 38 percent of Swedish households (Walker and Naeghele 2000). The largest component of household wealth in many countries is housing value. This value could fall if large numbers of older homeowners try to sell houses to smaller numbers of younger buyers. How successfully this transition is managed around the world could determine the rise and fall of nations and reshape the global economy in the era of the post-credit crunch. Two key vehicles of growth are increases in the labor force and productivity. If nation states cannot maintain the size of their labor forces by persuading older workers to retire later then the challenge will be to maintain growth levels. This will be a particular challenge in Europe, where productivity growth has averaged just 1.3% since 1995. By 2024, growth in household financial wealth in the U.S., Europe, and Japan will slow from a combined 4.5% annual reduction now to 1.3%. That will translate into $31 trillion less wealth than if the average age were to remain the same (Cook and Powell, 2007).

This also has an impact on older people, family and household. Indeed, older people's living arrangements reflect their need for family, community, or institutional support. Living arrangements also indicate sociocultural preferences—for example, some choose to live in nuclear households while others prefer extended families (Estes, Biggs and Phillipson, 2003). The number, and often the percentage, of older people living alone are rising in most countries. In some European countries, more than 40% of women age 65 and older lives alone (Walker and Naeghele 2000). Even in societies with strong traditions of older parents living with children, such as in Japan, traditional living arrangements are becoming less common. In the past, living alone in older age often was equated with social isolation or family abandonment (Phillipson 1998). However, research in many cultural settings illustrates that older people, even those living alone, prefer to be in their own homes and local communities (Gilleard and Higgs, 2001). This preference is reinforced by greater longevity, expanded social benefits, increased home ownership, elder-friendly housing, and an emphasis in many nations on community care

(Estes, Biggs and Phillipson, 2003). As people live longer and have fewer children, family structures are also transformed (Bengtson and Lowenstein 2004). This has important implications in terms of providing care to older people. Most older people today have children, and many have grandchildren and siblings. However, in countries with very low birth rates, future generations will have few if any siblings. As a result of this trend and the global trend toward having fewer children, people will have less familial care and support as they age (Bengtson and Lowenstein 2004).

As a consequence of the global demographics of aging, the changing societies of the post millennia are being confronted with quite profound issues relating to illness and health care, access to housing and economic resources including pension provision in Asia. Asian policy makers have to work beyond the nation state and create partners with other nation states to thwart the power of global aging from impacting on its ability to meet the needs of its population.

REFERENCES

Baker, H.D.R. (1979), *Chinese Family and Kinship*, London: Macmillan.

Beck, U. (1994), *The Risk Society,* London: Sage.

Beijing Review (1999), *Special Report on Falun Gong,* Vol. 42, No. 45, pp. 7-15.

Bengtson, V.L. and Lowenstein, A. (Eds.) (2004) *Global Aging and Challenges to Families*. New York: De Gruyter

Biggs, S. and Powell, J. (2000), 'Surveillance and Elder Abuse: The Rationalities and Technologies of Community Care', J*ournal of Contemporary Health,* 4, 1, 43-49.

Biggs, S. and Powell, J. (2001), 'A Foucauldian analysis of Old Age and the Power of Social Welfare', *Journal of Aging & Social Policy.*

Blecher, M. (1997), *China Against the Tides: Restructuring Through Revolution, Radicalism and Reform,* London: Pinter.

Britannica Book of the Year, 2001: World Data Annual, Chicago: Encyclopaedia Brittanica.

Building blocks (2004) *Africa-wide briefing notes – supporting older carers*, HIV AIDS Alliance and HelpAge International

Bytheway, W. (1995), *Ageism,* Milton Keynes: OUP.

Chen, S and Powell, JL (Eds.) (2011) *Aging in Perspective and the Case of China*, Nova Science: New York.

Chen, S and Powell, JL (Eds.) (2012) *Aging in China*, New York: Springer

China Daily (2004), *"Tailoring Health Care Policies for the Elderly"*, April 15th 2004.

Chinese Communist Party (1992/1995) *Decision to Speed Up Tertiary Industry. Central Committee Document,* No. 5, Appendix 3 in Yabuki, S., China's New Political Economy, translated by Harner, S.M.,Boulder, Colorado: Westview.

Cook, I.G. and Murray, G. (2001), *China's Third Revolution: Tensions in the Transition to Post-Communism,* Curzon: London.

Cook, I.G. and Powell, J.L. (2007) *New Perspectives on China and Aging.* Nova Science: New York

Deng Xiaoping (1981/1995), The Primary Task of Veteran Cadres is to Select Young and Middle-Aged Cadres for Promotion. In *Selected Works of Deng Xiaoping Volume II (1975-1982),* Beijing: Foreign Languages Press, Second Edition, pp.378-382.

Deng Xiaoping (1982/1995). Advisory Commissions Will be a Transitional Measure for the Abolition of Life Tenure in Leading Posts'. In *Selected Works of Deng Xiaoping Volume II* (1975-1982), Beijing: Foreign Languages Press, Second Edition, pp. 405-6.

Du Peng and Tu Ping (2000). Population Ageing and Old Age Security. In Peng Xizhe and Guo Zhigang (eds), *The Changing Population of China,* Oxford: Blackwell, pp. 77-90.

Epstein, H. (2001) 'Time of Indifference', *New York Review of Books,* April 12, pp.33- 38

Estes, C. (1979), *The Aging Enterprise.* San Francisco: Jossey Bass.

Estes, C., Biggs, S and Phillipson, C. (2003) *Social Theory, Social Policy and Ageing*. Open University Press: Milton Keynes

Fairbank, J.K. (1959), The Nature of Chinese Society, in Schurmann, F. and Schell, O. (eds), *China Readings 1: Imperial China*, Harmondsworth, Middlesex, UK: Penguin, pp. 34-46.

Federal Reserve Bank of Kansas City (2004) *Global Demographic Change: Economic Impacts and Policy Challenges. Symposium proceedings*. August 26–28, 2004. Available at:http://www.kc.frb.org/Publicat/sympos/2004/sym04prg.htm

Fitzgerald, C.P. (1976), *Mao Tse-Tung and China*, Harmondsworth, Middlesex, England: Penguin.

Foucault, M. (1967),. *Madness and Civilisation.* London: Tavistock.

Foucault, M. (1972), The Archeology of Knowledge, Tavistock: London.

Foucault, M. (1973). *The Birth of the Clinic.* London: Routledge.

Foucault, M. (1976) *The History of Sexuality.* Harmandsworth: Penguin.

Foucault, M. (1977) *Discipline and Punish.* London: Tavistock.

Foucault, M. (1980) *Power/Knowledge: Selected Interviews and Other Writings*, 1972-1977, New York: Pantheon.

Foucault, M. (1982) *The subject of Power.* In Dreyfus, H and Rabinow, P (Eds.) Michel Foucault: beyond structuralism and hermeneutics, Brighton: Harvester.

Foucault, M. (1984) *What is Enlightenment?* In Rabinow, P (Ed.) The Foucault Reader, London: Peregrine.

Frank, A.W. (1998), Stories of Illness as Care of the Self: A Foucauldian Dialogue, *Health*, Vol. 2, No. 3, pp. 329-48.

Gavrilov, L and Gavrilova, N (1991) *The Biology of Life Span: A Quantitative Approach.* New York: Harwood Academic Publisher

Giddens, A (1993) *Sociology*. Cambridge Polity Press

Giddens, A. (1991) *The Consequences of Modernity.* Cambridge: Polity.

Gilleard, C and Higgs, P. (2001). *Cultures of Aging*. London: Prentice Hall

Gittings, J. (1999). *Cult Descends on Heart of Beijing.* Guardian, 26th April.

Government of China (2002), *China Statistical Yearbook 2002*, China Statistics Press: Beijing.

Gruber J, and Wise DA, (eds.) (1999) *Social Security and Retirement around the World*. Chicago , IL : University of Chicago Press, 1999.

Gruber J, and Wise DA, (eds.) (2004) *Social Security Programs and Retirement around the World. Micro Estimation.* Chicago , IL : University of Chicago Press.

Guo, N. (2001), Plan Helps Seniors Enjoy Better Life, *China Daily*, 14th August.

Hadley, R. and Clough, R. (1996), *Care in Chaos*, Continuum International: New York.

Hansson, A. (1996), *Chinese Outcasts: Discrimination and Emancipation in Late Imperial China*, E.J. Brill: Leiden, The Netherlands.

Hansson, A. (1996), *Chinese Outcasts: Discrimination and Emancipation in Late Imperial China*, E.J. Brill: Leiden, The Netherlands.

Harper, S. (1994), China's Population: Prospects and Policies, in D. Dwyer (ed.), China: The Next Decades, Longman Scientific and Technical: Harlow, UK.

Heidegger, M. (1971), Poetry, Language, Thought, Harper and Row: New York.

Help the Age International (2000) *The Mark of a Noble Society*. London: HelpAge International.

Hermalin A, (ed.) (2002) *The Well-Being of the Elderly in Asia : A Four-Country Comparative Study*. Ann Arbor , MI : University of Michigan Press

Holtzman, R.A. (1997) *A World Bank Perspective on Pension Reform.* Paper prepared for the joint ILO-OECD Workshop on the Development and Reform of Pension Schemes, Paris, December.

International Monetary Fund. *The Economics of Demographics. Finance and Development. September* (2006) ;43(3). Available at: http:// www.imf.org/external/pubs/ft/fandd/2006/09/

Katz, S. (1996) *Disciplining Old Age: The formation of Gerontological Knowledge.* Charlottesville: University of Virginia.

Katz, S. (2000), Busy Bodies: Activity, Aging and the Management of Everyday Life, *Journal of Aging Studies*, Vol. 14, No. 2, pp. 135-52.

Kim, S., and Lee, J-W., (2007), "Demographic changes, saving and current account in East Asia", *Asian Economic Papers*, 6(2)

Kinsella K, and Velkoff VA. (2001) *An Aging World: 2001*. Washington , DC: National Institute on Aging and U.S. Census Bureau

Krug, E. G. (2002) *World Report on Violence and Health*. Geneva: World Health Organisation.

Li Yongping and Peng Xizhe (2000). Age and Sex Structures. In Peng Xizhe and Guo Zhigang (eds), *The Changing Population of China,* Oxford: Blackwell, pp. 64-76.

Liu, J. and Lin, F. (2000), Long-Term Effect of China's Family Planning

Longino, C. F. (1994). 'Pressure from our aging population will broaden our understanding of medicine'. *Academic Medicine, 72* (10), 841-847.

Lopez AD, Mathers CD, Ezzati M, Jamison DT, and Murray CJL, (eds.) (2006) *Global Burden of Disease and Risk Factors. Washington* , DC : The World Bank Group

Manton KG and Gu X. (2001) *Changes in the prevalence of chronic disability in the United States black and nonblack population above age 65 from 1982 to 1999*. Proceedings of the National Academy of Sciences 98;6354-6359.

Marx, K. and Engels, F. (1848/1985). *The Communist Manifesto*. London: Verso.

May, T. and Powell, J.L. (2008) *Situating Social Theory 2*. McGraw Hill: Maidenhead.

Merquior, J. (1985). *Michel Foucault,* New York: Fontana.

Murray, G. (1998), *China: The Next Superpower*, China Library: London.

Murray, G. (2004), *China's Population Control Policy: A Socio-Economic Reassessment,* PhD thesis, Liverpool John Moores University: Liverpool, UK.

Murray, G. (2004), *China's Population Control Policy: A Socio-Economic Reassessment,* PhD thesis, Liverpool John Moores University: Liverpool, UK.

Nathan, A.J. and Link, P. (eds) (2001), *The Tiananmen Papers*, Compiled by 'Zhang Liang', London: Little, Brown.

Organisation for Economic Cooperation and Development (OECD) Directorate for Employment, Labour and Social Affairs. (2007) *Disability Trends among Elderly People: Re-Assessing the Evidence in 12 OECD Countries* (Interim Report). Paris , France : OECD

Phillipson, C. (1998). *Reconstructing Old Age*. London: Sage.

Powell, J. (1998a) review of Katz, S (1996), Disciplining Old Age: The formation of Gerontological Knowledge. In *Acta Sociologica,* Vol. 41, No. 4, pp. 398-99.

Powell, J. (2000) *The Importance of a 'Critical' Sociology of Old Age.* Social Science Paper Publisher, 3, 1.

Powell, J. (2001), Theorizing Gerontology: The Case of Old Age, and Professional Power, *Journal of Aging and Identity, 6, 2 , 221-237*

Powell, J. and Biggs, S. (2000), Managing Old Age: The Disciplinary Web of Power, Surveillance and Normalisation. *Journal of Aging and Identity*, 5, 1, 3-13.

Powell, J. and Biggs, S. (2000), Managing Old Age: The Disciplinary Web of Powell, J. and Biggs, S. (2000), Managing Old Age: The Disciplinary Web of Power, Surveillance and Normalisation, *Journal of Aging and Identity*, Vol. 5, No. 1, pp. 3-13.

Powell, J. and Cook, I.G. (2000), "A Tiger Behind and Coming Up Fast": Governmentality and the Politics of Population Control in China, *Journal of Aging and Identity*, 5, 2, pp. 79-89.

Powell, J. and Cook, I.G. (2001), Understanding Foucauldian Gerontology: The Chinese State and the Surveillance of Older People, *International Journal of Society, Language, and Culture etc.*

Powell, JL and Cook, I (2010) *Aging in Asia*. Nova: NY

Powell, J.L. (2005) *Social Theory and Aging*. Rowman and Littlefield: Lanham.

Powell, J.L. (2009) 'Social Theory, Aging, and Health and Welfare Professionals: A Foucauldian "Toolkit", *Journal of Applied Gerontology,* 28, 6, 669-682

Powell, J.L. (2009) 'Social Theory, Aging, and Health and Welfare Professionals: A Foucauldian "Toolkit", *Journal of Applied Gerontology,* 28, 6, 669-682

Rabinow, P. (Ed.) (1984). *The Foucault Reader.* London: Peregrine..

Shumway, D. (1989). *Michel Foucault.* Charlottesville: University Press of Virginia.

Smart, B. (1985). *Michel Foucault.* London: Routledge.

Sun, X. (1996), *China's Social Security System*, Studies on the Chinese Market Economy Series, Gao S. and Chi F. (eds), Beijing: Foreign Languages Press

Tang, K-L (1999), Social Development in China: Progress and Problems, *Journal of Contemporary Asia*, 29, 1, pp. 95-108.

Tang, M. (2001a), Gov't Says The Elderly Should Not Be Forgotten, *China Daily*, 28th October.

Tang, M. (2001a), The Elderly - A Resource, Not a Problem, *China Daily*, 11th July.

United Nations Department of Economic and Social Affair (2002) *Population Division. World Population Ageing 1950–2050.* New York : United Nations.

Wahidin, A and Powell, J. (2001) The Loss of Aging Identity: Social Theory, Old Age and the Power of Special Hospitals. *Journal of Aging & Identity,* 6, 2.

Walker, A and Naeghele, G (2000) *The Politics of Ageing in Europe*. OUP: Milton Keynes.

World Bank (1994), *Averting the Old-Age Crisis*, Oxford University Press: Oxford, UK.

Yu, G. (1987), Spending the Remaining Years in Ease, in Women of China Special Series, *New Trends in Chinese Marriage and the Family*, Beijing: China International Book Trading Corporation, pp. 209-213.

Zeng, M. (2001), Elderly Chinese to Receive Better Care, *China Daily*, 22nd October.

Zhai Zhenwu (2000). The Population of China: Prospects and Challenges. In Peng Xizhe and Guo Zhigang (eds), *The Changing Population of China,* Oxford: Blackwell, pp. 246-256.

Zheng, L. (2004), China Faces Elderly Dilemma, *China Daily*, August 21.

INDEX

A

B

C

D

E

F

G

H

I

J

K

L

M

N

O

P

R

S

W